James Payn

The English Nation Identified with the Lost House of Israel

By Twenty-seven Identifications

James Payn

The English Nation Identified with the Lost House of Israel
By Twenty-seven Identifications

ISBN/EAN: 9783744757928

Printed in Europe, USA, Canada, Australia, Japan

Cover: Foto ©ninafisch / pixelio.de

More available books at **www.hansebooks.com**

THE

ENGLISH NATION

IDENTIFIED WITH THE

LOST HOUSE OF ISRAEL

BY

Twenty-seben Identifications.

DEDICATED
TO THE (SO-CALLED) BRITISH PEOPLE,
BY THEIR KINSMAN,

EDWARD HINE.

COUNTRY PUBLISHERS.

MANCHESTER: J. HEYWOOD. BIRMINGHAM: RICHARD DAVIES.
ABERDEEN; JAS. MURRAY.
EDINBURGH: J. MENZIES & Co. GLASGOW: JAMES McGEACHY.
BRIGHTON: H. & C. TREACHER. BRISTOL: WM. MACK.
BATH: B. PEARSON, MILSON STREET.
BRADFORD: J. F. HAMMOND. SHEFFIELD: HOPKINS & SON.
LEICESTER: WINKS & SON. LIVERPOOL: WILLIAM GILLING.

1871.

EPISTLE TO THE NATION.

MY KINSFOLK,

It is not my province to write a book.—I am without ambition that way; my great desire is to serve my country, giving forth such flashes of light to the people, as shall convince them that they are the Heirs to the greatest temporal, political and social blessings, our God has ever vouchsafed to any one particular and distinct Nation. Although throughout our history we have always occupied the most exalted position on the earth, yet the blessings that are now coming to us, are of a value far beyond what we have ever yet received. The very first that we shall inherit, is that of living in peace, entirely freed from the turmoils and convulsions of the Wars that are yet to engulf the Continent of Europe. With these Wars England will have nothing to do, we cannot be embroiled in them, they will last through some years, and while the other nations will be in the midst of sufferings, famines, and dire perplexities, we shall be enabled throughout this time, to live peaceably and without anxiety. God has said it, and His word is sure; we inherit these blessings by being Heirs to Israel, we are the very descendants of this lost people, in whom, so many valuable promises are vested. It has been the will of our God that we should be politically lost, until the latter days; we were not to be discovered until the times of the "wars and rumours of wars" had arrived. These times are now, this is the exact time specified by God for the political resurrection of Israel, effected in ourselves; they were to be "blinded" until the fulness of the Gentiles had come in; this has been fulfilled. That this time has come, is further proved by the restoration of the Latter Rain to Palestine. This rain was withheld for centuries, its Withdrawal, and the Captivity, being events that Solomon, in his prayer, connected together, and they return together; the rain is restored, and now Israel is found—found in ourselves. The time is now at hand when God has promised to bless us more largely than ever; we have not to wait for the Coming of the Lord, before he settles us after our "old estates" he will do this before our swords are beaten into plough shares. The positive promise that he "will do better unto us than at our beginnings," Ezek. xxxvi, 11, is almost immediate, we shall begin to realize this directly after we have effected our Identity Nationally, and it is of the utmost importance that this should be effected at once, as in these critical times of Warfare, it might save us from many grave mistakes. God will not effect it for us, without enquiry from us, Ezek. xxxvi, 37, therefore let the Church plead for it, it is our duty, it is vital to us, for when established, it is our Peace. The disciples were Israelites, of the tribe of Benjamin; that one tribe that was purposely left

behind to be a light in Jerusalem in the days of Christ.
I Kings xi, 13—32—36. Christ privately instructed these Israelites about the very times in which we now are. Matt. xxiv, 3.
They wanted to know about the latter days, and were told that
they would not be until "Ye hear of wars, and rumours of
wars, nation shall rise against nation, and kingdom against
kingdom, and there shall be famines, and pestilences, and
earthquakes." This was to be the lot of the Gentile nations, but not of Israel; we have no part in them, and
this is Christ's special instruction to our nation, when we
hear of these wars, "See that ye be not troubled," Matt.
xxiv, 6. Mark says the same, "Be ye not troubled," Mark,
xiii, 7. Luke says, "Be not terrified," Luke xxi, 9,
therefore let England build upon God's sure word, which has
never yet failed. These are instructions alone given to our
nation, it is impossible for the so-called English to be mixed
up with these quarrels, having other matters to attend to, our
Mission is to give testimony to the truth of the Bible, God
will call us to the front to be His witnesses. Is. xliii, 12, the nations in their troubles, will find out that they have followed after
vanities, and will flow to us, to be taught of the Lord, Jer. xvi, 19.
Grand and blessed times await our Identity. We have to claim
the land. The earth will be more productive to supply our wants
than before. The Lord will do better for us than at our beginnings. Then will be to us essentially times of peace, of gladness
and rejoicing. "When God bringeth back the captivity of his
people, Jacob shall rejoice, Israel shall be glad." Ps. liii, 6. It is
the climax of our national history; the ushering in of joyous
times.

In the foregoing, I simply hint at the grand temporal
and political blessings that God is now awaiting to pour
upon us when our Identity to Israel is seen by us. But my
primary object is the Glory and Success of the Church of
Christ; by this I do not mean Establishments, or Denomina-
tionalisms. Of these we have had enough, but the embodying
and consolidating of the Christians OF OUR LAND and
POSSESSIONS into ONE UNITED BODY; the bringing
about of that glorious time when we shall all see "EYE TO
EYE" with each other in the Service of GOD, and ALL
worship Him with "ONE CONSENT:" Ye that love
the Lord—this time can never arrive until AFTER Lost
Israel is recognised. I confidently challenge the learned of
our Country to produce a single passage from God's Word
promising such an event BEFORE Israel's discovery. It
cannot be—it is impossible—but it is faithfully promised to
us after the Identity. The same remarks apply to Missionary
Success.—We are not promised that the Gentiles will receive

the Glad Tidings of the Gospel before the political resurrection of Israel. Such a result would be directly contrary to what our Bible declares shall be ; ourselves, *i. e.* Israel as a Lost people, were commissioned first to preach the Gospel among all people AS A WITNESS ; this we have done, and have secured the only result that was ever promised to this WITNESS preaching, just a few believers in each nation, who have to testify our WITNESS was true. When Israel is restored —THEN and NOT BEFORE—will the Gospel make way through the earth. Then, and never before, will the Many Nations flow eagerly to Jerusalem to be taught of the Lord.

Therefore, Fellow Christians, the subject, seen in its Church aspect, becomes most important. You cannot fail ultimately to be enraptured with the subject, seeing the great glories you are seeking to realize can only come to you through it. But why delay ? Why not make the question a matter of enquiry AT ONCE ?

The late Professor Wilson introduced this subject some thirty years ago, in a work well worthy of perusal : "Our Israelitish Origin,"* really an invaluable book. He therein seeks to identify England with the tribe of Ephraim only, believing the modern nations North West of Europe to be the other tribes ; a view in which I perceive very great difficulty, but really so far as our nation is concerned, it makes not the slightest difference, for whether we are only a part, and that part the most favored tribe, or whether we compose the whole of the tribes, it is equally vital to us, and also of supreme importance to the interests of the Church of Christ in England.

Amongst numerous letters received, one is so admirably suggestive, and as I wish to awaken thought upon the subject generally, I annex it.

EDWARD HINE.

London, March, 1871.

Dear Sir,

I have read with much interest your Pamphlet on the " Identification of the English Nation with the Lost House of Israel." I cannot however but regret that you should have so limited the important question, instead of pointing out the wider scope it surely embraces ; for if the Anglo-Saxon race are of the House of Israel, it clearly follows that the whole of the German or Teutonic race, of which we form but a portion, however wide-spread and distinguished a portion, must be of the same origin.

* William Mackintosh, 24, Paternoster Row.

The English or Anglo-Saxons (though portions of other tribes, such as Danes and Normans, have been mixed up with them), constitute, I believe, the tribe of Joseph, the heir of the birth-right blessings (1 Chron. v. 1, 2.), the blessings pronounced by Jacob on the sons of Joseph, in that remarkable scene (Gen. xlviii.) recorded by the Holy Spirit as a special act of faith of the dying Patriarch. (Heb. xi, 21.) But foremost and pre-eminent in blessing as the seed of Ephraim and Manasseh were to be, the calling, privileges and destiny of Israel were also to be enjoyed eventually by the rest of the tribes, as implied in the closing words of Jacob's prophetic blessing: "In thee shall Israel bless, saying, God make thee as Ephraim and as Manasseh."

And do we not see this even now coming to pass in the rising power and influence of the Teutonic Nations, standing up, as a mighty great army, "the Empire of all Germany?" yet to embrace probably, or draw into closer alliance with itself other fragments of the same race on the Continent. The victorious career on which they have now entered is but the fulfilling of their mission as God's "battle-axe and weapons of war," to break and humble the Papal Powers, confederate with and so long the willing executors of the behests of Rome, the mystic Babylon "drunk with the blood of the Saints and the Martyrs of Jesus." But now, at the close of the predicted 1,260 years of her arrogant domination, the main supports and instruments of her evil policy are being broken by Israel, the great Protestant Power they have so long scattered and oppressed. With the overthrow of Austria in 1866 commenced the vindication of the wrongs done to them through centuries of wanton aggression and spoliation. This interference of God on their behalf is still more strikingly manifest by the utter prostration and humiliation of France, "the eldest daughter of the Church," in the conflict she so recklessly provoked, jealous of the growing power and union which her insolent challenge only tended the more speedily to establish, all Germany rising as one man to withstand their ancient and inveterate foe; and in the righteous judgment of God, after an almost unparalleled and unchecked career of victory (reminding of the triumphs of Israel of old), the foundation of her Empire has been laid on the very soil of the enemy, and inaugurated in the palace of the proud Monarchs who robbed her of the fair Provinces she has so successfully won back; no portion of Israel must be left in the enemy's grasp; therefore on the possession of Alsace and Lorraine hung the issue of the war: France compelled to relinquish her long hold of an integral portion of German territory which she had acquired by fraud and violence.

Surely at so striking and important a crisis in the history
of Europe, however thankful we may feel for our present
immunity from the horrors of War, it behoves us as a nation
to uphold the righteous cause with all our moral influence, and
to rejoice in the signal triumph of our brethren of Israel.
Protected and prosperous in our insular position, "separated
by the deep that coucheth beneath" from our brethren on the
Continent, as the tribe of Joseph was to be, the English Nation,
like their favored progenitor (in whose personal history theirs
was so remarkably pre-figured), are called to exercise their
high and happy privilege of ministering from their ample
store, life, health and blessing to all, whether of alien or
kindred race; yet it is their wisdom and duty especially to
cultivate a closer and hearty friendship and alliance with their
brethren, the tribes of Israel. Satan well knows the significance
of such an alliance. His aim, therefore, is to mar and hinder
it, by stirring up the worldly, papistical and infidel elements in
our midst, in order to draw us into closer affinity and sympathy
with Babylon and her principles, their hearts lingering in her
cities of pleasure, whence have flowed the corrupting influences—
social, political and religious—which have defiled our land and
people. But rebuke and judgment must follow, unless shaking
off the yoke of Babylon, and resisting her meretricious attrac-
tions, we draw into closer bonds, political and national, with
those whose arms are being strengthened by the God of Israel
to accomplish His purpose amongst the nations.
The recognition of our, and their identity with the Lost
House of Israel should lead to a more distinct manifestation of
our oneness, this our manifested union being so closely connected
with the great events of the latter days, ushering in the return
of the King of Israel, David's son and David's Lord, to take
His believing people unto Himself, and to establish His kingdom
of peace and righteousness on earth. Even now in the midst of
the din of war and clash of arms, and the pouring out of the vials
of God's wrath on the apostate Nations, faith anticipates that
day, and whilst His judgments are made manifest, is able to
re-echo Heaven's solemn note of praise, saying: "Great and
marvellous are Thy works, Lord God Almighty; just and true
are Thy ways, Thou King of Nations."

Believe me,

Yours truly.

Heads of Identities.

4

The English Nation Identified

WITH

THE LOST TRIBES OF ISRAEL,

BY

TWENTY-SEVEN IDENTIFICATIONS

BASED UPON SCRIPTURE.

Two Great Questions have for many generations puzzled and set at defiance the intelligence of the great and learned of our land. The first, What has become of the Lost Tribes of Israel? The Second, Who were the ancestors of the English People?

The object of these pages is to show that the latter are identical with the former, and out of very many others that could be produced, to advance Twenty-seven Identifications that shall clearly establish the proposition. A few introductory remarks are needed. We take for granted that the reader is well informed as to the past Israelitish history,—that they were once One People, and afterwards became Two Houses: the House of Israel, and the House of Judah. Since their captivities this distinction of the two houses becomes the grand essential to be borne in mind. To confound Judah with Israel and Israel with Judah, is the root of all mistakes in reference to this subject; these two peoples are as distinct as France from Russia, as fire from water, so that to speak of Israel as meaning the Jews, is to fall into an error, which destroys the sense and meaning of much of the prophetic word : yet this mistake is almost universally made, the result being, that in the pulpits of our divines the prophetic word is seldom touched upon; the great command to "take heed" to the sure word of prophecy is disobeyed, or, if brought forward at all, it is generally so wrested, by its literal meaning being disregarded and a spiritual one substituted, that from a dozen different pulpits a dozen different interpretations are given; and under this teaching the word can no longer be said to be the "*Sure* word." (2 Peter, i. 19), or be taken as the "light that shineth in a dark place." It is quite contrary to the spirit of prophecy, when a plain literal interpretation can be accepted, to substitute a figurative or spiritual one. "No prophecy of the Scripture is of any private interpretation," and the greater number admit of a literal sense. Thus, with the Jews, or the House of Judah, it is most interesting to mark how literally the prophecies have been, and are still being carried out. Thus,—"I will cause thee to serve thine enemies in the land which thou knowest not." Jer. xvii., 4. "And I will deliver them to be removed into all the kingdoms of the earth for their hurt, to be a reproach and a proverb, a taunt and a curse in all places whither I shall drive them." Jer. xxiv., 9; Jer. xxix., 18. "I will fan them with a fan in the gates of the land; I will bereave them of children." "Thy substance and thy treasures will I give to the spoil without price." Jer. xv., 7 "Thou shalt not prosper in thy ways; and thou shalt be only oppressed and spoiled evermore, and no man shall save thee;" "and thy life shall hang in doubt before thee, and thou shalt fear day and night and shalt have none assurance of thy life." Deut. xxviii. 29, 66.

These and many other dreadful curses have been literally fulfilled, and to this day in our own country the Jew is a taunt, a hissing, and a by word. Then surely if they have been so minutely fulfilled with the one House, so surely shall a literal fulfilment take place of the prophecies concerning the House of Israel. Very many of these have been fulfilled most wonderfully, yea marvellously; indeed so many, that but few are left yet to be accomplished, and these few must shortly come to pass. The most remarkable feature of the prophecies concerning Israel, is their exactly opposite character as contrasted with those concerning Judah. Thus, instead of being a marked people, known by all nations, Israel was to become a lost people, known by none, not even to themselves. Hosea i. 9; ii. 17. Instead of being a small people, bereft of children, Israel was to have the multitudinous seed as the "stars of heaven." Instead of being a dispersed people, and no nation, Israel was to become a fulness of nations, kings coming out of her. Instead of being a trembling people, smitten before her enemies, Israel was to be the most warlike nation, possessing the seat of power, "the gate of her enemies." Instead of being a standing witness to the prophetic word, Israel was to become the overwhelming witness to the truth in the Latter Times. Instead of being under the Mosaic Law, Israel was divorced from the Law and is to be found in Christ. Judah is represented as Deaf, but Israel as Blind. It was treacherous Judah. Backsliding Israel. From Judah one seed. Of Israel seeds, and so forth. Israel was never Judah, but Judah was *of* Israel, and will, eventually, be one with Israel. Sometimes Judah is referred to in Scripture as of Israel, when the distinction is still kept up, for then Israel as the Ten Tribes is distinguished as "All Israel," "the whole House of Israel," the "House of Israel wholly," &c. These distinctions are more generally to be found in the Book of Ezekiel.

A review of the leading prophecies concerning Israel, will enable us most clearly to identify the English people as the Lost House of Israel.

IDENTIFICATION THE FIRST.—THE CAPTIVITY.

It was not until 725, B.C. that Israel or the ten Tribes was carried captive by Assyria, "and the King of Assyria did carry away Israel unto Assyria, and put them in Halah and in Habor by the river of Gozan, and in the cities of the Medes; because they obeyed not the voice of the Lord their God, but transgressed his covenant." 2 Kings 18, 11, 12. It was in these parts that Israel was lost, which includes the southern border of the Caspian Sea, and as far west as Araxes, beyond the Euphrates. Here her name was to be taken from her, "they shall no more be remembered by their name." Hos. 2, 17. Hitherto they had been known by the name of God's people "My people." "Then said God, call his name Lo-Ammi,"

Hos. 1, 9, meaning "not my people." They were only to be lost in name, they were to be "blinded," become ignorant of their ancestry, and as this "blind" people, were yet to accomplish the marvellous works allotted to them as the "preordained" "chosen" and "special" seed. "Yet doth he devise means that his banished be not expelled from him," 2 Sam. 14, 14. "And I will bring the blind by a way they knew not; I will lead them in paths they have not known," Is. 42, 16, thus Israel though in captivity, inasmuch as they were "cast out" of their land, yet would not remain under the dominion of the Assyrians, for God twelve years after the event says through Nahum "though I have afflicted thee, I will afflict thee no more. For now will I break this yoke (the Assyrian) from off thee and will burst thy bonds in sunder. Nahum 1, 12, 13. This the prophetic word plainly recognises as having been done, for afterwards Israel is addressed as being in the North, and then North West of the seat of Prophecy: "Behold these shall come from far, and lo, these from the north, and from the west." Is. xlix., 12. "To the islands will he repay recompense, so shall they fear the name of the Lord from the west." Is. lix., 19. "Go and proclaim these words towards the north, and say, return thou backsliding Israel." Jer. iii., 12. That Israel did not go to the East, is positive, because God in prophecy declared they should have "the Assyrians before, and the Philistines behind." Is. ix., 12. Had they gone eastward this would have been reversed; therefore, this assures us they went first to the north, then to the west, which is further proved by the direction Paul went when he journeyed after them, and Christ himself never went to the south of Jerusalem, where the Jews were chiefly to be found, but always to the north, through Samaria. Had his mission been to the Jews, he would have gone southwards, but he did not.

Thus it be evident that from this point they would become wanderers, without any fixed design of their own, whether their tribeships would be kept as distinct as they were when in the Land, I am not prepared to affirm, though I think the probability is that they would endeavour so to preserve them, at least for a time.

Since the publication of the former Editions of this work. I have been amazed to find the amount of ignorance that exists upon the Captivity of Israel, having been told, even by Ministers who presumably should know better, that Israel did return, they confounding Israel with Judah, and the 70 years, that I must be allowed the indulgence now and then of shewing the difference of the two Houses; Israel never returned, they went into captivity 725 B.C.; Judah went into captivity 588 B.C.; but Israel at this time was in captivity, and had been so for 134 years. Israel's captivity was in Assyria; Judah's in Babylon. Israel's was complete, "there was none left but the tribe of Judah only." 2 Kings, xvii., 18. Judah being then a distinct nation. Judah's was partial, the poor being left behind. Jer. xl., 7. Israel never returned, their captivity "is unto this day." 2 Kings xvii., 23. Judah did return after the 70 years. Neh. vii., 6.

THE IDENTITY. In just such a state as that of these people now, were our ancestors found. The Anglo-Saxons were wandering tribes among the Germans, with so much of the warrior spirit, that the Ancient Britons invited them into these isles to help them in their national difficulties. To trace the origin of our forefathers has been the perplexing problem for ages. Who were the ancestors of these Anglo-Saxons? To this day nationally we are in positive ignorance as to our true ancestry, a mystery which these pages are intended to remove. From the very parts through which the tribes of Israel wandered, we came. So interesting has been the tracing of our ancestry to our historians, that to some it was a life study. Sharon Turner is foremost in the search, and he traces us to the very spot where Israel was carried captive, the one where the name of Israel was taken from them. Arriving here, he loses all further trace of them. Here was the connecting link, but had he seen and lain hold of it, the purposes of God would have been frustrated, for the "time of the end" was not then come, for which reason was it hid from him. The fact however, is most important, and forms the ground-work of our argument. Our own historian, Sharon Turner, in treating of the second or Teutonic stock of European population in his "*Anglo-Saxons*," (vol. i., 93—102) says, "It is peculiarly interesting to us, because from its branches not only our own immediate ancestors, but also those of the most celebrated nations of modern Europe, have unquestionably descended. The Anglo-Saxons, Lowland Scotch, Normans, Danes, Belgians, Lombards and Franks have all sprung from that great fountain of the human race, which we have distinguished by the terms Scythian, German, or Gothic." "The first appearance of the Scythian tribes in Europe may be placed, according to Strabo and Homer, about the eighth,* or, according to Herodotus, in the seventh century before the christian era." "The first scenes of their civil existence, and of their progressive power, was in Asia, to the east of the Araxes.† Here they multiplied and

---

* The date of the Assyrian Captivity.

† The identical part into which Israel had been carried captive.

extended their territorial limits for some centuries, unknown to Europe." The account of Diodorus is, "That the Scythians, formerly inconsiderable and few, possessed a narrow region on the Araxes; but, by degrees, they became more powerful in numbers and in courage. They extended their boundaries on all sides; till, at last, they raised their nation to great empire and glory. . . In the course of time they subdued many nations between the Caspian and Mœotis, and beyond the Tanais." "In the time of Herodotus they had gained an important footing in Europe, and to have taken a westerly direction." Having reference expressly to the Saxons. Sharon Turner observes, "They were a German or Teutonic, *i.e.*, a Gothic or Scythian tribe; and of the various Scythian nations which have been recorded, the Sakai, or Sacae, are the people from whom the descent of the Saxons may be inferred, with the least violation of probability. They defeated Cyrus, and reached the Cappadoces on the Euxine. That some of the divisions of this people were really called Sakasuna is obvious from Pliny; for he says that the Sakai who settled in Armenia, were named Sacassani, which is but Saka-Suna, spelt by a person who was unacquainted with the meaning of the combined words. . . . It is also important to remark, that Ptolemy mentions a Scythian people sprung from the Sakai, by the name of Saxones."

These extracts are invaluable to our purpose, as they call to our aid Strabo, Homer, Herodotus, Diodorus, Pliny, and Ptolemy to prove that our so-called Saxon ancestors came from the parts where Israel was lost, making their first appearance in those parts at the exact time that Israel was lost—two most important points, by which we are enabled to gather another most important fact, viz., that in the days of Christ our forefathers were then occupying the north-west of Asia, and gradually making their way into Europe; that in the very days of the Apostles our race were located in Cappadocia, Galatia, Pamphylia, Lydia, Bithynia, Mysia, Achaica, Thessaly, Macedonia and Illyricum. We are traced in this direction seven hundred years before Christ, and we did not reach these isles until 430 years after Christ; so that between these periods and at the time of Christ we were in the regions specified. This is important to see, because one of Christ's most pronounced declarations was, that He was "not sent but unto the lost sheep of the House of Israel." Matt. xv., 24. He instructed his disciples, saying "Go not into the way of the Gentiles, and into any city of the Samaritans enter ye not, but go rather to the lost sheep of the House of Israel." Matt. x., 5. And, in obedience to this command, we find the apostles making their journies to the precise localities where our English forefathers then were, preaching the word and forming churches.

This is an indisputable interesting historical coincidence, which fully justifies the inference of an Identity.

IDENTIFICATION THE SECOND.—"THE ISLES."

After Israel's captivity, after they had freed themselves from the Assyrian yoke, and after their wandering in a blind state in the north west of Europe, the sure word of Prophecy which cannot fail, plainly intimates that their course would be directed to "the Isles," "the isles afar off."

"Keep silence before me O Islands." Is. xli., 4. "The Isles shall wait for His law." Is. xlii., 4. "Sing unto the Lord a new song—the Isles and the inhabitants thereof." Is. xlii., 12. "Listen, O Isles, unto me." Is. xlix., 1. "Hear the word of the Lord, O ye nations, and declare it in the Isles afar off, and say, He that scattered Israel will gather him, and keep him." Jer. xxxi., 10. These all refer to Israel; and there are many more that testify that Israel would locate themselves in the Islands north west from Palestine, the seat of prophecy, and when they reached these Islands would have to accomplish great and arduous missions only given to them, and of a nature so grandly gigantic and expansive, as would become utterly impossible for any other nation on earth to accomplish, and the positive and literal accomplishment of which become the fruit by which they shall be known.

It must be borne in mind that all the Israelites were not literally carried into captivity by Assyria, for a remnant of them escaped. (Obadiah 14). The captives were carried to the north, the remnant that escaped went southwards, by the Mediterranean Sea, consequently there was a great distance between the two bodies, and one would not know the movements of the other. Yet God's design was to bring them together, those in the south would, by a different route, be sent to the "Isles afar off," for in Is. lxvi., 19, it is said, "I will send those that escape of them unto the nations," "to the isles afar off."

THE IDENTITY. Presuming that the tribeships would have been kept distinct, that they would have conducted their wanderings in separate bands, and so at different periods have entered these British Isles, which are certainly afar off from the seat of prophecy, and in a north-westerly direction; this would exactly tally with the mode that our forefathers actually made their appearance here, and would furnish us with the reason why they made ten distinct migrations at various times, and at different points into this country. If Israel did this, of course being blinded, they would only be known as Gentiles, and those that escaped would not enter Britian by way of Germany or Denmark as most of our forefathers did, but through France as the direct way from the Mediterranean, and would thus account for our Gauls and Normans. This much is certain that if Israel had been kept in tribeships up to the point of their reaching the isles, afterwards this distinctiveness would not have been preserved but would merge into one great nation being always addressed as one united people, just as our ancestors ultimately became. Of course this theory revolutionizes our popular acception of English History, that of being a mixture of ten different people from whom have come the mightiest Nation on the face of the earth, which is most vague, and by no means plausible; nay more, such a theory after a careful consideration is most unsatisfactory as it conveys a cruel reflection on the word of the Almighty, which is tantamount to a direct insult to our God, inasmuch as we, ': so-called English, have accomplished without one excepti a, (thus far) every mission God so faithfully promised should come forth from Israel, whereas no other nation has touched them, and it is now an utter impossibility for any other people to do so. Therefore our old theory would make it appear that God had substituted another Nation in the place of Israel to bring forth these Marvellous Works, which are the Glory of the Almighty God, whereas he has distinctly promised that He would not take His Glory away from Israel, and give it to another people. God says "For mine own sake, even for mine own sake, will I do it. For how should my name be polluted? And I will not give my glory unto another." Is. xlviii., 11; No! "God is not a man that he should lie, neither the son of man that he should repent, hath he said, and shall he not do it? or hath he spoken, and shall he not make it good?" Num. xxiii., 19. "I am the Lord: that is my name: and my glory will I not give to another, neither my praise to graven images." Is. xlii, 8. This promise is not given to Judah, but only to Israel, and was sent after them when they were living in the Isles.

IDENTIFICATION THE THIRD.—RENEWING STRENGTH.

Israel, after their wanderings through the north-west, and their settlement in the isles afar off, were to "renew their strength." Though a warlike people from the first, still their wanderings, with the conflicts that would result as they passed through the lands of strangers, would greatly enfeeble and impoverish them, this was the case before they crossed the Jordan to possess the land, when they had the special and visible tokens of God's help, how much more so now, when apparently they were left entirely to themselves, every new passage through fresh country would be by might, not by right, every inch of ground gained would be by the use of the bow; work not of a day, but of generations and would be the cause of much weakness and fatigue.

But when the isles are reached prophecy comes forth with her edict, and says—"Keep silence before me, O Islands; and let the people renew their strength." Is. xli., 1, giving as a reason in the 8th verse, "Thou Israel art my servant. Jacob whom I have chosen, the seed of Abraham, my friend." And saying in the 10th verse, "I thy God, I will strengthen thee."

THE IDENTITY here with the English nation is so plain, that it is needless to enlarge further than to bring out the fact, that we did exactly what Israel was to have done, that is, renewed our strength. The Saxons had been for years in the north-west parts of Europe before their coming into Britain, as likewise the Gauls in France, for one of the reasons why Julius Cæsar invaded England was, that the Britons had assisted the Gauls in their battles against his armies, and the last Roman légion sailed from England 475 years after Cæsar had landed, most of this time was one of warfare, and of depopulation, but mark how wonderfully have we increased since then.

IDENTIFICATION THE FOURTH.—STARS OF HEAVEN.

There were three grand birthright promises made to Abraham, but that of the multitudinous seed, is the only one we notice here. That this was to be literally a national seed as distinguished from other nations, is most clear, from the careful way in which God himself preserves its descent. Abram was lamenting that he had no seed, and says, "Lo, one born in my house is mine heir, and the word of the Lord came unto him saying: This shall not be thine heir, but he that shall come forth out of thine own bowels shall be thine heir. And he brought him forth abroad, and said, look now toward Heaven, and tell the stars, if thou be able to number them. And He said unto him, so shall thy seed be." Gen. xv., 3-6. Great care was made to confirm this promise to Isaac,—Gen. xxvi., 4, as also to Jacob—Gen. xxviii., 14. Jacob, who was afterwards called Israel, had twelve sons, representing the twelve tribes, and that there should be no doubt as to whom out of the twelve should inherit this promise of the multiplicity, we find that Joseph, whose name means Increase, was to be a "fruitful bough," saying, "The blessing of thy father have prevailed above the blessings of thy progenitors, unto the utmost bound of the everlasting hills. They shall be upon the head of Joseph." Gen. xlix., 26. We then find the promise descending most minutely unto Ephraim, saying, "And his seed shall become a multitude of nations." Gen. xlviii., 19. Thus it is most plain, that after the separation of the twelve tribes into two houses, the inheritance of the promised multitudinous seed was with Israel, now the lost house, and not with Judah. For at the very time of their captivity, at the time when God was withholding his name from them, that they should become a lost people upon the earth, at that exact time God ratifies his ancient promise, saying, "Yet the number of the children of Israel shall be as the sand of the sea, which cannot be measured nor numbered." Hos. i., 10. "Unto Judah was given the sceptre," Gen. xlix., 10, "from whom the lion of the tribe of Judah should come," the *one* seed Christ, so very beautifully distinguished from the "seeds as of many," by Paul. Gal. iii., 16. Now to Abraham and his seed were the promises made. "He saith not, and to seeds, as of many; but as of one, and to thy seed, which is Christ." Indeed, the multiplicity could not be with Judah, otherwise the promises would go for naught, and prophecy have failed (which is impossible) for the Jews, inheriting their curse, do not increase to draw forth remark, not now being nine millions strong in all the countries of their dispersion, numerically insignificant in comparison with other nations, therefore this fulness of nations must now be on the earth, they cannot be hid in a corner, they must have intercourse with other nations, and be identical with some powerful nation, whose origin is obscure, making THE IDENTITY so plain with our own immense nation, that it is needless to enlarge, and will become more plain in the other Identifications.*

IDENTIFICATION THE FIFTH.—A MONARCHY.

In connection with the promise of the multiplicity, is one having reference to Government, for in the first edition of the promise given to Abraham, it is said, "Kings shall come out of thee." Gen. xvii., 6. And again shewing the importance of this promise, we have in Gen. xxxv., 11, "And Kings shall come out of thy loins." This promise was also given to his wife the Lord saying, "Sarah shall her name be, and I will bless her, and she shall be a Mother of Nations; Kings of People shall be of her," Gen. xvii., 16, and let it not be said that this was fulfilled when Israel was in the land. It was not. None of the promises were fully realized when Israel was there, she not having full possession of the land according to the promise. It was in her captivity that the Monarchy, and Nations would be fully accomplished. So that in searching for lost Israel, this should be an important consideration, for wherever they are, they must be under a monarchy; therefore could not be the Jews, who have no king, or government of any kind of their own, nor could they be a small people, such as the Nestorians, not being a recognised power,—nor still more an uncivilised tribe such as the North-American Indians. Prophecy makes it also very plain that after their captivity, after their wanderings and their settlement in the isles—after they had lost their children through fatigue and warfare, and while yet feeling themselves captives, moving to and fro, and even after the renewing of their strength with "the children which thou shalt have, after thou hast lost the other," that then in this primeval state "Kings shall be thy nursing fathers, and their queens thy nursing mothers," Is. xlix., 23. So that soon after their settlement in the isles, after they had become a people lost as to name, they would be under a strong government in the form of a Monarchy, one able to protect them, and make them a people to be feared by other Powers.

THE IDENTITY. This is just the state of things appearing in our early history. Directly after our strength was sufficiently renewed, and we were able to throw off the Roman yoke, Egbert, the so-called Saxon, was chosen as king, and from him has descended the most powerful Monarchy the world has ever known, with its power supreme in action to the present day.

IDENTIFICATION THE SIXTH.—THE STRAIT.

So inconvenient was the possession of the multitudinous promise to be to Israel after her settlement in the isles, because of the vastness of the increase of her population, that there would be no room for her full developments. The isles were to become too small for her rapid growth. Thus we have prophecy telling us in Is. xlix., 19, concerning Israel, that "the land shall even now be too narrow by reason of the inhabitants," and in verse 20 they cry, "The place is too strait for me, give place to me, that I may dwell."

THE IDENTITY. Our forefathers soon found themselves in the same circumstances as these Israelites were to be, and had not other countries been opened up to us, it would have been difficult to say what would have become of us. One of our very greatest national blessings was the discovery of America, and though the fulness of a nation has already come forth from us there, still, in our present day, we have reason to cry in Britain. "The place is too strait for us;" and the fact should quicken our national activities in schemes for a large emigration, on a scale that shall be sensibly felt in our over-crowded cities.

IDENTIFICATION THE SEVENTH.—COLONIES.

One great and grand mission that was given only to Israel to accomplish was the filling up or peopling of the waste places of the earth. She is likened unto "a fruitful bough by a well, whose branches run over the wall." Gen. xlix., 22. In Is. 49, where Israel is specially addressed as in the "Isles," we have that beautiful "Thus saith the Lord, in an acceptable time have I heard thee, and in a day of salvation have I helped thee; and I will preserve thee, and give thee for a covenant of the people, to establish the earth, to cause to inherit the DESO-LATE HERITAGES;" verse 8. And then as they go forth from the isles to these waste lands, God promises to shew them the way, to "lead them," to "guide them," removing all difficulties from their way, saying, "I will make all my mountains a way, and my highways shall be exalted." Thus God most plainly intimates that he had provided Colonies for the convenience of the multitudinous seed to come forth from Israel. He fore-saw the horrors always resulting from an overcrowded Country. He heard their prayer for more room, and tells them he had opened up New Countries for their use, implying that some would lay in Torrid Zones, for he says "neither shall the heat nor sun smite them." The same idea is again expressed in Is. 54, where Israel is represented under the figure of the divorced woman and Judah the married wife," for more are the children of the desolate, than the children of the married wife saith the Lord." Then she is told to make use of the provision made for emigration, "Enlarge the place of thy tent," lengthen thy cords and strengthen thy stakes, for thou shall break forth on the right hand, and on the left, and thy seed shall inherit the Gentiles and make the desolate cities to be inhabited." It was in this way that Israel would be sown in the earth, as the Lord says, "And I will sow her unto me in the earth." Hos. ii., 23. "They of Ephraim shall be like a mighty man, they shall increase as they have increased, and I will sow them

among the people, and they shall remember me in far countries." Zech. x., 8, 9. Then surely Israel must be found in
no unimportant position on the earth. It is utterly an impossible thing that she be a small people, as the Jews really are.
She must be a nation, with colonies of extraordinary growth,
and these in all parts of the world; for she was to spread
abroad, "to the west, and to the east, to the north, and to
the south." Gen. xxviii., 14. And at the time of the restitu-
tion, from these quarters will she be gathered, and that this
shall be accomplished we have the emphatic warrant of Scripture, which now is saying to literal Israel, "And behold I am
with thee, and will keep thee in all the places whither thou
goest, and will bring thee AGAIN into this land; for I will not
leave thee, until I have done that which I have spoken to thee
of." Gen. xxviii., 15.

THE IDENTITY. It may truly be said that no other
nation but the English have done anything towards a real filling
up of the waste places of the earth, and it is also a most remarkable and indisputable fact that at the time the above prophecies were given, the only "desolate heritages," then in
existence that could claim the prefix of the definite article,
were America, Canada, Australia, New Zealand and South
Africa. St. Paul testifies that Italy and Spain, and indeed
the Continent of Europe, were in possession, and History
affirms the same with Asia; so that it becomes patent that the
"desolate heritages" or Colonies that God has declared he had
provided only for Israel, have all of them, one by one come
under the dominion of our rule. Therefore, if Israel was to do
this, and the English is the only nation that has done it, the
identity is self-evident, and unless we see this fact, and connect
with it the great reason why they were provided for us, because
of the multiplicity of our race, it is impossible for us to understand the precise relationship or uses of our Colonies to these
British Isles, or for us to entertain any adequate idea of the
immense advantages embodied in Emigration. I maintain that
this is the only correct light in which to see the great questions
of Colonial management and Emigration, and unless laid hold
of, our Colonial Office will be constantly repeating the mistakes
they have made, and our Colonial Minister still enjoy his
apparent luxury of being continually in hot water and perplexity.

IDENTIFICATION THE EIGHTH.—THE UNICORN'S HORN.

One great characteristic that must be discovered in Israel
will be her pushing propensity. The idea given is, that when-
ever she acquires new country for her own use, that the original

possessors, or the aborigines of that country, will be pushed as by the "horns of Unicorns," that with them "he shall push the people together to the ends of the earth, and they are the ten thousands of Ephraim." Deut. xxxiii., 17. The same idea is given by the Psalmist in writing about Israel, xliv., 4 and 5, "Thou art my King, O God, command deliverance for Jacob. Through Thee will we push down our enemies."

THE IDENTITY. We need only give a few instances to shew that this characteristic is most remarkably possessed by the English people. In our own country we have the Welsh descended from the ancient Britons, pushed into a corner of the country once their own, and subject to our rule. The same may be said when our sons went forth to America, there we have the Indians pushed into the back-woods of that country, the same thing will be found in Canada and Australia, with the maories of New Zealand, and the Caffres of the Cape.

IDENTIFICATION THE NINTH.—ISRAEL A CHRISTIAN PEOPLE.

Wherever Israel shall be recognised, she must be found preeminently a christian people. When God caused her to be lost, it was done by simply taking away her name, by which act a blindness happened to her, that she became ignorant of the stock from which she had sprung; but though not called by His name, and ignorant herself of her own ancestry, God never intended to forsake her, but still to accomplish by her the purposes he had designed,—thus, at the very time he took her name away he made her a promise, saying, "I will be to them as a little sanctuary in the countries where they shall come." Ezek. xi., 16. Can He be said to have been this to the Jews? this were impossible, until they turn their face to acknowledge their Saviour. The Jews, or Judah are under the Law, Israel is not. She is now, and must be found a people entirely free from the Mosaic covenants, not regarding the Mosaic rites, either in worship, sacrifices, or circumcision. Lost Israel has been completely divorced from this ceremonial law. Judah is not. This distinction is so plainly made to us by God. "And I saw, when for all the causes whereby backsliding Israel committed adultery I had put her away, and given her a bill of divorce, yet her treacherous sister, Judah, feared not." Jer. iii., 8. "Thus saith the Lord, where is the bill of your mother's divorcement, whom I have put away?" Is. l., 1. Thus, a divorced woman, she becomes "desolate" and "forsaken," and that we may know that Israel was this

desolate forsaken woman, we are told of the multitudinous
seed. " For more are the children of the desolate than the
children of the married wife, saith the Lord." Is. liv., 1. Paul
saw this when speaking of the allegory of the two covenants,
and says, " The desolate hath many more children than she
which hath an husband." Gal. iv., 27, The whole gist of his
argument being that the Galatians should free themselves as
Israel had done, from the Judaising ceremonials, and " stand
fast " in the liberty of Christ. That they must now be taught
in Christ is manifest, for this was Christ's mission. " I am not
sent but unto the lost sheep of the house of Israel." Matt.
xv., 24. That Christ would have no part in spiritualizing away
the " Sure word," but meant the literal seed is equally manifest by his first, earnest instructions to his twelve disciples.
" Go not into the way of the Gentiles, and into any city of the
Samaritans enter ye not; but go rather to the lost sheep of the
House of Israel." Matt. x., 5. It was unto Israel God spake,
" For the Lord hath called thee as a woman forsaken, and
grieved in spirit. For a small moment have I forsaken thee,
but with great mercies will I gather thee." Nay, Israel must
now be literally a distinct national seed, waiting on God and
believing in Christ, a people on whom God is bestowing his
grace in a measure beyond what he is doing unto other nations.
" Ephraim also is the strength of mine head." Psalm lx., 7.
" The isles shall wait upon me, and on mine arm shall they
trust." Is. li., 5. " And it shall come to pass, that in the
place where it was said unto them, ye are not my people there
it shall be said unto them, ye are the sons of the living God."
Hos. i. 10. Paul says the same " There shall they be called
the children of the living God." Rom. ix., 26. " I said not
unto the seed of Jacob, seek ye me in vain." Is. lxv., 19.
" Israel shall be saved in the Lord with an everlasting salvation." Is. xlv., 17. " Shew the house of Jacob their sins, yet
they seek me daily, and delight to know my ways, they take
delight in approaching to God." Is. lviii., 2. " The Redeemer
shall come to them that turn from transgression in Jacob, saith
the Lord." Is. lix., 20. " Arise, shine for thy light is come,
and the glory of the Lord is risen upon thee." Is. lx., 1.
" Though Israel be not gathered, yet shall I be glorious in the
eyes of the Lord, and my God shall be my strength." Is.
xlix., 5. " The Lord sent a word into Jacob and it hath lighted
upon Israel." Is. ix., 8; Is. li., 7; Is. lxiii., 8; Ps. xxii., 23;
Jer. xxxi., 18-20; Hos. ii., 23. " The Kingdom of God shall
be given to a Nation bringing forth the fruits thereof." Matt.
xxi., 43. " Blessed be the Lord God of Israel, for he hath
visited and redeemed his people." Luke i., 68. " To remember His holy covenant, the oath which He sware to our father

Abraham, that He would grant unto us, that we being delivered out of the hand of our enemies, might serve him without fear, ... to give knowledge of salvation unto his people." Luke i., 73 74. These are all given to Israel, not one refer to Judah, and many other passages if we had room to produce them, testify to Israel being a Christian people; as to Judah, so far from her being in Christ, it is vain to expect it for some years to come, it would be contrary to Scripture, Christ who came from Judah, "came to his own, but his own received him not;" hence their rejection. Many times it is said, God would not hearken to them. Zeck. vii., 13. They will return to the land under the Mosaic law, and will there re-establish the Temple Service or chapters of Ezekiel 40 to 47 ending twelfth verse mean nothing; and men who solicit subscriptions in aid of Jewish conversions will almost invariably be found quoting Scripture referring only to Israel, and applying it to Judah, simply because no such texts exist for Judah. It is money thrown away, as facts themselves prove. It is only in the latter days that Judah will turn to Christ. Zeck. xii., 10, and not until then will the two sticks become one: though both will be in the Land, still the Law (Mosaic) will go forth from Zion, "and the word of the Lord (Gospel through Israel) from Jerusalem." Mic. iv. 2. "Let God be true, but every man a liar." Rom. iii., 4.

THE IDENTITY. That the English have been more highly favoured with divine light above any other existing nation, has long been acknowledged. As a nation we are almost alone in being able to worship God according to our conscience, sitting under our own vine and fig tree, none daring to make us afraid. God has literally been to our people a sanctuary, and our lands are filled with his houses. Truly as a nation we may be said to have been exalted unto the heavens by our special privileges. He hath not dealt so with any other people. Indeed it is most pointed to remark, being, if not an identity, a most marvellous coincident, that in the time of our Saviour and his apostles our Saxon forefathers were not then in possession of Britian, but were wandering, in tribes, along the north-west of Europe and Asia (as proved by our own great historian, Sharon Turner), coming from the very parts where Israel was lost, and proceeding to the very parts that prophecy says Israel would take; that it was, when we were in these parts, that Christ sent his own disciples to them, that is,—that when the apostles were sent after lost Israel, they went to Cappadocia, Galatia, Pamphylia, Lydia, Bithynia, and round about Illyricum; and it was in these very parts that our Saxon forefathers were passing through at this very time. With such light, the Lord may well say, "Who is blind but my servant?"

IDENTIFICATION THE TENTH.—
DENOMINATIONAL SECTS.

Though prophecy has declared that Israel in her Captivity should become a Christian Nation, it as plainly declares that the people should not be united in their religious opinions, but should be divided into Sects, and be known under Denominational Names. The prophecies contained in the forty fourth of Isaiah, which were given to Israel, 712 B.C., or about thirteen years after their captivity (and 124 years before the captivity of Judah) promises assurances of favour, saying, God "will help thee;" though in captivity they were not to fear upon this point, for they were yet the chosen Nation, and whoever among the people became "thirsty," desiring to be God's, such should be watered; upon such, God would pour His Spirit, and give His blessing upon their children; that the time was coming when these watered ones should "spring up as among the grass, as willows by the water courses." Yet there would not be a thorough union in their Christian views, for "One shall say, I am the Lord's; and another shall call himself by the name of Jacob; and another shall subscribe his hand unto the Lord, and surname himself by the name of Israel." Is. xliv., 5. Thus their different Churches, called by various names, would represent the opinions of each Sect. God declares this shall be the case with Lost Israel, and when they are nationally recognised, this shall be an identity; yea, this very division God says He is Himself going to call forth as a Witness to the Majesty of His Almighty Being, saying "Have not I told thee from that time," the time "since I appointed the ancient people that these things should be," "that are coming, and shall come," and that shall shew the marvellous foreknowledge of the Most High; even Christ himself declared that there should be divisions on account of religion, and this can only refer to the time during which Israel is lost, for after her discovery we shall have no bigotry, no priestly assumptions, for it is this very discovery, her very identity, that leads to the time of which God speaks, when he says of Israel, that "with the voice together shall they sing, for they shall see eye to eye, WHEN the Lord shall bring AGAIN Zion," Is. lii., 8, which most plainly implies, that now, during the present time there does not exist a oneness of heart with Israel.

THE IDENTITY of our Nation on this head is most pointed. The diversity of opinion upon religious subjects is really painful to behold; perhaps on no other topic are we so much at variance with each other. The church stamped with the Nation's name, is cut up into sections, oppressed by divisions; churches that are surnamed by the name of men, suffer under the same affliction, and churches called after the name of the Lord, still want much of the spirit of their Master. This is a most humiliating aspect of our Church History, plainly testifying that our very church life is under captivity. The very Heathen in their idol worship are more united, they have different idol gods, but there is more uniformity in the method of worship. All sincere lovers of our Lord must deplore division, and should be found ready at the very earliest moment to seek a remedy to cure the evil. It can never be done by Evangelical Alliances, or Christian Unions; these can only shew a desire for union, indicative that the time is close at hand for its enjoyment, but can never effect it; it can only be done by God's own means, and that is by our National Identity. It is one of the practical uses of my subject, and I call upon all Christians who earnestly desire the unity of the Spirit to act with wisdom, use God's means; remember it is nowhere promised until AFTER the Identity of Israel, God faithfully promises after our recognition to "take away all the detestable things," "and all the abominations," saying, "I will give them one heart." Ezek. xi., 19. The passage already quoted, Is. lii., 8, says the same thing, it is AFTER the Identity, not before. "For THEN will I turn to the people a pure language, that they may ALL call upon the name of the Lord, to serve Him with ONE CONSENT." Zeph. iii., 9. Surely, my fellow Christians, if there were no other blessing to obtain from our Identity, this alone would be invaluable; the most blessed service ever yet rendered to the Church. And Brethren, be not deceived, the enjoyment of this oneness of heart and opinion does not imply the immediate dawn of the Millenium; it shall be ours to possess before this grand Age, for Israel shall dwell many years safely in her Land, before our Lord shall come in Glory. Ezek. xxxviii. 8. This we are distinctly promised, and God cannot lie, though the teachings of many of our Divines have appeared to make him out unfaithful, yet Glory be to God, He is not. We shall have this union of heart, we shall reclaim possession of our Land, and when there the Gentile Nations shall flow to us to be taught of the Lord; this alone will occupy some years, and there are other great events that will in themselves be a work of time, and that must be accomplished before the appearing of our Lord, and though men have uttered error against the Lord by saying that He will not come, yet He will as surely come as we shall be Identified, the Spirit be poured out upon us, living as Christians in the royal law of love and unity, and that before He comes, which is not so immediate as some have led us to suppose.

IDENTIFICATION THE ELEVENTH.—SUNDAY SCHOOLS.

Israel in captivity, in her lost estate, must be distinguished from all other Nations of the earth by the fact that she must have a careful solicitude that her children should be taught in the Lord. God distinctly declares that this shall be the case with Israel, whereas I do not find that He has given the same instructions to any other Nation. Israel went into captivity 725 B.C., if the Chronology of our Bibles is correct. I find that in 698 B.C., or 27 years after the captivity, and while Judah was still in the land, that the Lord sends this after Israel " As for me, this is my covenant with them, saith the Lord ; My Spirit that is upon thee, and My words which I have put into thy mouth, shall not depart out of thy mouth, nor out of the mouth of thy seed, nor out of the mouth of thy seed's seed, saith the Lord, from henceforth and for ever." Is. lix., 21. Similar passages are to be found given before the children possessed the land, but I produce this to shew that the promise was not cancelled by the punishment of captivity. " I will pour My Spirit upon thy seed, and My blessing upon thine offspring." Is. xliv., 3. " All thy children shall be taught of the Lord ; and great shall be the peace of thy children." Is. liv., 13. Israel only is here addressed, not Judah ; the very next verse says she should be established in righteousness, and be far from oppression, whereas Judah was to be oppressed, which is a fact of the present day. Thus Israel must be a Nation that brings up her children in the knowledge of the Lord.

THE IDENTITY says that the English race are the only people so doing. Sunday Schools especially provided for the training of our children in the Lord, exist with us, and our race as a National Institution, perhaps the greatest in point of blessing that we possess ; true they are modern in origin, still our forefathers in their more primitive ages were always particular in the religious training of their children, and reared some of the finest examples we have of Christian endurance and fortitude. It was only as the population increased, and poverty among the masses became more abundant, that the organisation of Sunday Schools became a necessity. Of our present population nearly seventy per cent. may be said to have passed through our Sunday Schools, Charity Schools, and Ragged Schools. In America the proportion is greater. Among the Upper and Middle classes, another twenty per cent. have been trained in the home circle in the Lord, so that we may safely say that ninety per cent. of the entire people have been taught of Christ. God does not work by miracles in these days, He works by the use of means, He has faithfully promised after our Identity is accepted by the Nation, to pour out His Spirit upon us as a people; the ground is already prepared for this out-pouring, the instructions given by the Christian teachers are merely latent, "train up a child in the way he should go, and when he is old he shall not depart from it." We are not told there shall be no departure from the training, between the period of childhood, and old age; the reverse is implied, and the large mass of the ungodly testify that departure is a fact. Alas! alas! too apparent; still, Sunday School teachers, you are not to be discouraged in your work, present results are not your promises, your great reward is future. I believe that Sunday Schools have been raised up purposely for the event of our Identity, and is the reason why they were not in existence over 70 years ago. The Lord is only waiting for our National anxiety to be Identified. We are to "give Him no rest until," &c. The matter is really in our hands; promulgate the truth of the Identity. God's promises are sure, He has only to breathe upon this prepared soil, and the masses of the people will declare for God, it will be no miracle, simply the workings of God's law of Nature, and then will be the harvest, and the fruit of all Sunday School labor. Teachers, is there not a power for you to use in this subject? Be worthy of your vocation, it is in the power of nearly all of you to realise the positive reward of your past toil in your own lifetime. You are the real power of the Church. Your Thought has led the way in many Questions. You cannot forget how you have achieved great things, notwithstanding opposition. We must remember that many of our ministers have publicly committed themselves to grave mistakes in Bible renderings, as a learned Divine expressed himself in my hearing recently; many of them have been too eager to appear to have found out what is not written, that they might seem to be abreast of an advanced age, and obtain a false fame for their scholarship. Experience has always testified that human nature is not too fast to acknowledge the committal of a mistake; therefore wait for no one, the Bible is common property, belongs to us all, and is as accessible to our understanding as to anybody else's; therefore, teachers, go to it, see for yourselves that these things be, and only abide by God's word, if you see therein these statements are facts; take the matter in your own hands, send it through the Nation like wildfire, and very soon it shall come to pass, that the Williams's and James's, your Martha's and Mary's whom you remember to have taught in your Infant Schools, but who now, in the prime of their lives, are found by millions in the haunts of vice, shall once more pay heed to your voice, their early associations of your faithful labors in their school life shall be revived in their memories, and they shall in masses return to our God as your harvest, your reward. God has promised this, and He is ever faithful.

IDENTIFICATION THE TWELFTH.—"ANOTHER TONGUE."

Abundant Scripture evidence has been advanced to prove that Israel in captivity would receive the Gospel tidings, and be established as a Christian people. My next object is to shew that she would not receive these Gospel truths or teach them to her children in her original, or Hebrew language. God only refers to Israel, and not to Judah, when He says, "With stammering lips, and another tongue will He speak to this people." Isa. xxviii. 11. Therefore it be plain that after the Assyrian captivity, Israel would acquire another speech, foreign to that she had used when in the land.

THE IDENTITY of ourselves to Israel, which is surely established, would render this point most striking. We have acquired a new speech, and it is "another tongue" to that used by our forefathers which the masses of our kindred read their Scriptures in. It is not too much to say that there are not more than one in every two hundred thousand of our race who understand the Hebrew language, a remark that cannot apply to Judah, for the very children of the Jews are instructed in Hebrew, and are trained to read their Old Testament Scriptures in that tongue.

We do not wish to underrate scholarship, but it is a remarkable fact that our most learned linguists have been singularly unfortunate in their interpretation of Scripture. We should be very sorry to understand the Old Testament as the Jews interpret it, who resort to the old tongue; and the very churches in our midst who pride themselves most in being able to secure the services of scholars in Hebrew and Greek, really have made the least progress, seem to have the least light, and are the most inactive in home and foreign missionary operations. We have most faith in God's Word. He said He would speak to us in "another tongue, and in this, the "another tongue," we have been the most successful and triumphant, and have secured Christian vitality and spiritual health in the largest degree.

IDENTIFICATION THE THIRTEENTH.— PHYSIOGNOMY.

When Israel became a lost people, not only was she not to be known by her speech, but also by the cast of her features.

To suppose that she would be recognised by her physiognomy is most illogical. If we wanted any person or thing to be placed in obscurity for a given time, we should obliterate all traces in disguise, or be chargeable with folly. Surely God would not be less wise than ourselves. If He had set a mark upon Israel, as He has done upon Judah, He would have defeated His own purposes—this very mark would have led to identity, as it has done in all countries in the case of the Jew. God has nowhere said that Israel should be known by her features—the idea is not given in the Bible. The supposition testifies to an incomplete knowledge of Scripture. God has only placed His mark upon Judah. It is of Judah only that it is said "The shew of their countenance doth witness against them." Is. iii. 9. Nay, that the very reverse would be the case of Israel we have a clear type in Joseph, who, after he was sold in captivity, after only a few years' absence, was not recognised, either by voice or feature, by his own brothers.

THE IDENTITY need not be further extended. The Saxon or English race do not bear the Jewish cast of face; it is right that they should not. Whether we really bear the Israelitish stamp I am not so clear, for hitherto we have taken a false notion of Israel—we have been looking for them through the Jew, whereas the Jews are not Israel, but simply "of Israel." It may turn out that we have the Israelitish feature, which is not the Jewish; and it may be, even with the Jews, that their present features materially differ from what they had before they inherited their curses, for this very mark is one of the curses. They had it not in Babylon, for though there in captivity, they were not under the curses, which did not overtake them till their second, or Roman captivity, after their rejection of Christ. Queen Esther in Babylon was not known as a Jewess. Esther ii. 10.

IDENTIFICATION THE FOURTEENTH.— THE MISSIONARY WORK.

Israel was not only to be a Christian nation with her children taught in the Lord, but to her alone, of all the people of the earth, has been entrusted the great and glorious Missionary work. She cannot help being a missionary people, for God has decreed that she should be. It is her work, and she must be found true to her mission, for it is impossible for The Book not to be true. The missionary work has been entrusted to Israel, but most certainly not unto Judah : it would be nonsense to expect to find Judah's heart in the missionary cause; it is a fixed decree of the Almighty that she remain under the Mosaic Law during her captivity, and even when she returns to the Land—when she is placed there by Israel—even then will Judah be for a time under this Law; but Israel, the Christian nation, who remains in captivity until she comes to a knowledge of herself—this Israel, even in captivity, must abound in the work of the Lord; it is one of her birthright promises that Christ came not to destroy, but to confirm. Matt. v. 17. The missionary work was confided to her before her possession of Palestine: "In thee shall all families of the earth be blessed." Gen. xii. 3. "And in thy seed shall all the nations of the earth be blessed," Gen. xxvi. 4. Christ, who came from Judah (Judah being his own tribe), is the one seed in whom all living souls can be saved, but the seed of Israel—the "seeds, as of many."—are to be the medium of conveying the glad tidings of this Saviour.

Christ came to His own, but His own (tribe) received Him not. "Therefore," said Christ, "say I unto you, the kingdom of God shall be taken from you, and given to a NATION bringing forth the fruits thereof." Matt. xxi. 43. So the work was alone entrusted to Israel. She by no means forfeited this high and holy prerogative by her captivity. Prophecy is most clear upon this point, as the following passages given after this event will shew : "Israel shall blossom and bud, and fill the face of the world with fruit." Is. xxvii. 6. "I, the Lord, have called thee in righteousness, and will hold thine hand, and will keep thee, and give thee for a covenant of the people, for a light of the Gentiles." Isa. xlii. 6. "This people have I formed for myself; they shall shew forth my praise." Isa. xliii. 21. "Thou art my servant, O Israel, in whom I will be glorified." Isa. xlix. 3. "I will also give thee for a light to the Gentiles, that thou mayest be my salvation unto the end of the earth." Isa. xlix. 6. "And their seed shall be known among the Gentiles, and their offspring among the people; all that see them shall acknowledge them, that they are the seed which the Lord hath blessed." Isa. lxi. 9. "And I will strengthen them in the Lord; and they shall walk up and down in His name, saith the Lord." Zech. x. 12. "O, bless our God, ye people, and make the voice of his praise to be heard." Psalm lxvi. 8. Israel was told what to say unto the heathen through Jeremiah: "Thus shal. ye say unto them, the gods that have not made the heavens and the earth, even they shall perish from the earth." Jer. x. 11. "And the remnant of Jacob shall be in the midst of many people as a dew from the Lord, as the showers upon the grass." Micah v. 7. "And your eyes shall see, and ye shall say The Lord will be magnified from the border of Israel." Mal. i. 5.

All the Gospels testify to the same fact. Christ tells us that He came after lost Israel, and says that all Scripture must be fulfilled, saying, "I have given them thy word." John xvii. 14. And alone speaks of Israel as the missionary people when He says "Neither pray I for these alone, but for them also which shall believe on me through their word." John xvii. 20. Surely nothing could be plainer than that Israel must be the great missionary people of the earth.

THE IDENTITY must be established on this point. Our race alone have the great missionary work in hand. We alone of all the nations have positively and literally obeyed Christ's commands by preaching the Gospel "in all the world for a witness unto all nations." Matt. xxiv. 14. Both in England and America, Christians of each denomination endeavour to vie with each other in this glorious work. Our missionary societies are the glory of both lands, and of our Colonies; each are in receipt of enormous revenues, and represent a world of zealous energy. In no other department of labour have our kindred displayed more courageous daring, determined boldness, and matchless bravery, than our men who, single-handed and undefended, have risked their lives in the cause of the Lord in missionary work. The so-called valour we have been taught from our childhood to admire in military men, pales when compared with the valour of the missionary. I fail to discover any real courage displayed by the soldiers of our forefathers when they marched round Jericho. The work was always done for them. It was always a question of mere blowing of rams' horns. They could not help succeeding; God willed it, and they had little more to do than to butcher runaway men as the war terminated in their favour, that the spoil might be greater and their pockets filled by the division of the prize-money. And all our wars ever since have been on a par. Bravery cannot consist in slaying fugitives. But the case of the missionary is quite another thing—here is valour. He braves odds fearfully against him; positively throws himself before the very teeth of cruel and wild savages who have looked upon the white man as a rich dainty. Dr. Livingstone to wit, who, unaided by a single European, has fearlessly marched thousands of miles in the very thick of an unknown, unexplored country, daring to face tribes of man-eaters with the open Bible in his hand, and besides Moffat and Williams, we have a host of others who shall answer "here," when God shall shortly call over the muster roll of the missionary army. Yes, we only are in possession of this work that was only given to Israel to undertake, and thus we are furnished with another evidence that we are identical with that people. If we are not, then most

assuredly, wherever Israel must be at this present time, she
would be foremost in this great work, and her seed would be
known among us, for she would make both England and America
and all our Colonies her missionary stations. If we are not
Israel—then wherever Israel may be, she would have translated
the Bible from her language into ours for our own special use
by her own Bible Society; she would have inundated our land
with tracts and gospel books from her own Religious Tract Society, she would have built for us churches and chapels throughout the length and breadth of the British Isles, and surely
with our universally recognized advanced civilisation, she would
have taken especial care to have cut up our country into Bishop-
rics, and Ecclesiastical Districts; she surely would not be less
foolish than Rome in such a matter as this. But no Nation is
doing this for us, Germany sends to us her missionaries of infidelity, and Rome, which has ceased to be a Church, became a
mere French machine immediately the French troops entered
the confines of Italy. She is now simply a French instrument
in the hand of God, to raise the ire of the Greek church, who
will be the means of swamping Rome entirely in a few years
hence, so that we have no Nation sending missionaries to us.
Therefore if we are not Israel, and Israel wherever she be is not
doing this for us, then the Bible is not true, but a fabrication
from beginning to end, and the many passages I have quoted
stand for nothing, without meaning; but this is impossible;
every word of the Bible is true, and the very fact that we in
blindness have accomplished without one exception every mission given to Israel irrevocably stamps every word as true, and
witnesses that God is God. Is. xliii., 12. "Let God be true,
but every man a liar." Rom. iii., 4.
    And now, reader, may I say there is a fearful responsibility
resting upon you, after reading this one Identity? The whole
Missionary Work now rests upon this subject. It is utterly impossible to secure the universal knowledge of the Lord, until
lost Israel be recognised. God has not given a single promise
of such a blessing in the entire Bible, until AFTER our Identity, it is not until then that the Gentile and Heathen Nations
will flow to Israel to be taught of the Lord; therefore to go to
our churches and pray, as we constantly do, for the prevailing
knowledge of God, and ignore the Identity of Israel is merely
hypocrisy. God Himself says that He will be enquired of by
the House of Israel to do it for them, He commands us to give
Him no rest until He makes Jerusalem a praise in the earth;
therefore, to sincerely desire the universal knowledge, implies
the use of means, we must each seek to have our Nation Identified, it cannot come before; but God has faithfully promised
that it shall be after. The Gospel was first to be preached as

a witness to all Nations; this we have done, there does not exist a nation where we have not published it. We now only wait for the political resurrection of Israel, "For if the casting away of them be the reconciling of the World, what shall the receiving of them be but life from the dead?" Romans xi., 15. My subject might save millions of money now spent in missionary work if the Identity was speedily effected, because after this event we reverse the order of proceedings; instead of our sending the Gospel out to the people, the Nations themselves will come to us. God has said it, and no man dare deny it. "The Gentiles shall come unto thee from the ends of the earth, and shall say surely our fathers have inherited lies, vanity and things wherein there is no profit, and they shall know that my name is the Lord." Jer. xvi., 19. "God shall bless us, and (afterwards) all the ends of the earth shall fear Him." Ps. lxvii., 7. "The Heathen shall know that I am the Lord God WHEN I shall be sanctified in you before their eyes." Ezek. xxxvi., 23; Is. ii., 2-3; Mic. iv., 1-2; Is. xi., 9; Hab. ii., 14; Is. lv., 5; Is. lx., 2-12; Is. lxii., 2-4; Is. lxii., 10-12.

The day has now arrived when it no longer rests with the missionary to secure this long prayed for result, but with our Identity. Why is not this grand discovery in the hands of the Clergy. Mr. Wilson, a layman, gave the key note to this great subject more than 30 years ago, why have not the ministers taken the matter up? Why should the subject still be in the hands of a layman, and why should it be left to the congregations to force the question into the pulpit, when it should have been there from the first? Let but the church take the matter up, and seven years hence we could wind up the affairs of all the Missionary Societies in existence, dating them with things of the past, and even now it would be a justifiable and wise economy on the part of our large hearted wealthy Christian merchants, to give their thousands in promulgating the truth of this Identity, which alone is to effect the crowning success of all missionary labor, rather than to the Societies. It would be a wise economy, saving millions. I say again the Gospel has been published AS A WITNESS unto all nations, its universal acceptation is nowhere promised until after lost Israel repossess her land, which repossession can only be secured by her Identity being known and established.

IDENTIFICATION THE FIFTEENTH.—
PHILANTHROPY.

Still continuing the cry "where is the lost house of Israel," and how shall they be found? We must answer, "by their

uits ye shall know them," and under this heading we will give
nother description from Scripture of Israel in addition to the
any already given. Wherever she be, her religious element,
hich shall be found largely to predominate, and be infused
to all her Institutions, shall stamp her as having a kind and
umane heart. I wish to be understood; to speak only of what
hall come forth from her religious convictions, because politi-
ally, as represented by her Government, I find that until she
ecomes nationally Identified the reverse would be the case.
srael politically and commercially, as distinct from her better
nd religious life, will be found loving to oppress. Hos. xii. 7.
ut religiously she shall be found as a power throughout the
orld, uncompromisingly the hater of oppression, the unflinch-
g opponent of despotism and tyranny, a people having a
hristlike sympathy with all kinds of distress, and a manly and
enerous hand ever ready to relieve suffering. Her country
ould be a free asylum, a city of refuge for the persecuted and
e exile, and to her, and her alone, has been entrusted the holy
ission of the abolition of slavery; It was Israel and not
udah, who was told to undo the heavy burdens, and to let the
ppressed go free, by no possibility could this mission be given
Judah; for she was to be a servile people, serving her
nemies in all countries, Jer. xvii. 4. It would therefore, be
bsurd to suppose that Judah, herself oppressed, could let
he oppressed go free. God is reasonable and never enjoins
n impossible service from any people. It was after Israel
ad left the land, that the Lord found them fasting for
trife, and debate and rebuked them. These fasts evidently
ationally prescribed were not such as God desired, therefore
Ie thus instructed them: "Is not this the fast that I have
hosen? to loose the bands of wickedness, to undo the heavy
urdens, and to let the oppressed go free, and that ye break
very yoke? Is it not to deal thy bread to the hungry, and that
ou bring the poor that are cast out to thy house? when
ou seest the naked that thou cover him; and that thou hide
ot thyself from thine own flesh? Is. lviii. 6-7.

THE IDENTITY. In Philanthropy no Nation has taken
e strides that the English race have. We have enjoyed the
ree essentials, and employed them, the power, the will, and
e means, and under the examples of such noble pioneers as
lizabeth Fry, Howard, Wilberforce, Buxton, Thompson,
orster, Pease, Brougham, and a host of others of greater and
sser lights, we have sacrificed millions, and achieved wonders
n behalf of oppressed peoples, nor have our sons in the New
Vorld been behind in the work, under the influence of the
aching of such men as William Lloyd Garrison, Wendle
hillips, Elihu Burritt, and Abraham Lincoln, they were led

to have compassion for the bonds of slavery, and waged the most dire and complete war that has ever been fought, at the cost of immense wealth and streams of blood, that they might burst those bonds asunder. Can we not also point to stately buildings positively teaming throughout our land, many of them magnificently endowed by the hand of benevolence, whose doors are opened to suffering humanity. At home or abroad, in countries our own, and not our own, when a real necessity presents itself our hand is opened to assist, so that this identity must be considered complete. The only thing that might seem to mar its completeness is that scandal to England, the mode of poor relief in this country, where poverty is treated as crime, where our Unions are generally made as uncomfortable as possible, the officials selected for their excelling in harshness, and heavy rates squandered upon interests that do not administer to the comfort and well being of the poor in their declining days. But this abomination springs from our political, which is apart from our better life, and the time is at hand when our Nation shall no longer be governed by party Spirit, but by Bible principles. Goshen is a town of Judah, and interpreted means "approaching," "drawing near," therefore let us see an omen, that the oppression of the Poor Law Board is "drawing near" to a close. We have no business with much poor in England. The Bible says so, Deut. xv. 4, and we have to thank our Governments for most of the pauperism and poor rates that they have indulged us with. I shall have to recur to this matter specially, but must say here that if we only took the advice of Florence Nightingale, and sent forth our poor to till God's earth in the millions of acres that He has given us for this express purpose, and that are now, to our shame, and to the disgrace of our Government, lying waste, in a few years we could sweep pauperism entirely away and abolish the devil-born term, and along with it the Poor Law Board and its iniquities. Let but the cash that is now wasted upon Privy Seals and objectionable sinecures be diverted to this channel, and then we shall be able to say that the real welfare of the Nation is studied. Surely, true Statesmanship would see wisdom in doing this voluntarily, rather than have to pass through the mortification of having to do it by the pressure of opinion, or resigning office as unprofitable servants.

IDENTIFICATION THE SIXTEENTH.—
THE ARMY.

As the grandeur of our subject opens up to the mind of the English Nation, perhaps, no point will take them so much by surprise as that of the Army. Most certainly there are but few topics that will more plainly testify to the masses of the people the unerring sureness of God's word. The Bible as handled by our ministers has been divested of so much of its beauty, by its national, political and social aspects, being almost entirely submerged under the one ruling thought of their mind, by which everything is turned to a spiritual account, that the political subjects of the Book, comprising a volume in themselves, have been toned down and abstracted, by their having been made to give way to spiritual applications; thus we are distinctly told in Scripture that Israel, after she was lost, would become the most powerful Nation on earth; would have the first and best Army in the world; and that by their soldiers they would not only obtain a "Balance of Power," but positively have lordship, become dominant, and exercise authority over the Gentiles; and this subject, given forth to the people in its entirety, its purity, and proved before them, would have revited their attention, and have gained their admiration for our grand old Bible, as a book of truth; but with a class of men, when God speaks to our Nation and tells us that we should "possess the gates of our enemies," they at once turn aside its natural and true meaning, by saying that God simply means that souls in Christ should possess mastery over the devil, and so it is not to be wondered at that under this everlasting spiritual mutilation, applying every iota of the Scripture to the soul, soul, soul, that the book has ceased to be interesting to so great a proportion of our population. The vindication of God's sure and precious word is higher in purpose, and in duty, is a more Divine purpose of life than the salvation of a human soul! The Majesty of God's word must ever be esteemed a more important matter, than the well-being of his children! "Let God be true if thereby every man becomes a liar." Rom. iii. 4. Nay, may we as a people ever desire to esteem God, before we esteem ourselves, knowing that it is only as He is glorified, that we ourselves can share His Glory, let us take Him at His word; dreading to "add unto" or to "take away from" the words of the prophecy of this book; so that when He says Israel shall be warlike, we may be quite sure that He means it, in the matter of powder and shot, bayonet and sword, and not simply warriors for truth; therefore, in looking for Lost Israel we must find her "Chief of the Nations" in the art of war, still maintaining her ancient character, that of being "terrible from the beginning hitherto." Is. xviii. 7. This is Israel's birthright, of which she has never been divested, and it is impossible that any nation can be identified with her unless so found; she must be foremost in power. "By myself have I sworn, saith the

Lord," unto Abraham, "thy seed shall possess the gate of his enemies" Gen. xxii. 17, and when Rebekah was blessed it was said, "let thy seed possess the gate of those which hate them" Gen. xxiv. 60. Unto Jacob it was said, "let people serve thee, and nations bow down to thee; be lord over thy brethren." Gen. xxvii. 29. The Gate was the Seat of Government—the Cabinet—to possess which was to conquer, to defeat; Israel of old always effected this by the instruments of war, the spear, the bow, and battle axe, and in these days would be found using this power by the more modern appliances; by no means did she forfeit this perogative by the punishment of her captivity, she must still be chief in military matters, because 13 years after their captivity, this was sent after Israel, "thou art my servant; I have chosen thee, and not cast thee away," * * * "they that war against thee shall be as nothing," Is. xli. 9-12, 27 years after, God says to Israel, "For the nation and kingdom that will not serve thee shall perish," Is. lx. 12, and 130 years afterwards, God says to Israel, and not to Judah, "Thou art my battle ax and weapons of war: for with thee will I break in pieces the nations, and with thee will I destroy the kingdoms." Jer. li. 20. Luke saw this truth, and records "That we should be saved from our enemies, and from the hand of all that hate us, to perform the mercy promised to our fathers; the oath which he sware to our father Abraham." Luke i. 71. There are many other passages to prove the fact, that Israel must be, by the will of God, chief in war, making **THE IDENTITY** so plain that it is needless to dilate, or pages might be consumed by the bare mention of our conquests. Interesting accounts of many of them may be found in a work recently published, entitled "A Synoptical Account of the GREAT EUROPEAN BATTLES."* I have no delight in war, therefore forbear to treat further on this head. If I proceeded it would be with the object of detracting from the merits of the long boasted daring and bravery of our officers and men, which we have so unduly been called upon to admire. We readily grant that we have some few individual cases where real courage has been displayed, but generally there has been no need for courage. We have gone forth confident of victory; the raw recruit, the mere clod-hopper from the field has been sufficient for the service. God has willed that we should triumph, without the exercise of daring or feats of bravery. He Himself has said so, and I take Him at His word, for in speaking to Israel about her wars He distinctly says, "Thou shalt be far from oppression; for thou shalt not fear: and from terror; for it shall not come near thee." Is. liv. 14. And this is why inexperienced

*Simpkin, Marshall & Co.

he gate of his
was blessed it
se which hate
t people serve
thy brethren."
ernment—the
defeat; Israel
var, the spear,
e found using
means did she
captivity, she
3 years after
u art my ser-
y." * * *
Is. xli. 9-12,
and kingdom
and 130 years
, "Thou art
will I break
roy the king-
cords ".That
the hand of
our fathers;
Luke i. 71.
e fact, that
var, making
to dilate, or
of our con-
v be found in
al Account
ve no delight
head. If I
g from the
officers and
dmire. We
s where real
een no need
ry; the raw
n sufficient
ph, without
self has said
Israel about
om oppres-
it shall not
experienced

young men are found sufficient to officer our regiments,
whereas other powers require men of judgment. I do not
speak of our civil wars here, for as in the days when our
forefathers were in the land, real bravery would be required
for these, and we have always displayed it in such wars, and
never was it more fearfully manifested upon any part of the
earth, than by our sons across the water in their recent
conflict with each other; but as to our wars with other
Nations, the great fear that our men have suffered under has
been from the woful blunders of our War Office officials
in the peaceful abode of Pall-Mall; but in positive war, David's
experience has always been ours, "Through thee will we push
down our enemies; through thy name will we tread them
under that rise up against us, for I will not trust in my bow,
neither shall my sword save me, but thou hast saved us from
our enemies, and hast put them to shame that hated us."
Ps. xliv. 5. "Ascribe ye strength unto God, His excellency
is over Israel;" "the God of Israel is He that giveth strength
and power unto His people." Ps. lxviii. 34. "Through God
we shall do valiantly; for He it is that shall tread down our
enemies." Ps. cviii. 13. Of Israel it is said, "Who if he go
through, both treadeth down and teareth in pieces, and none
can deliver; Thine hand shall be lifted up upon thine adversaries, and all thine enemies shall be cut off." Mic. v. 9.

IDENTIFICATION THE SEVENTEENTH.—
THE NAVY.

It being so indisputable that Israel must be the most famous
Nation in army matters, and having such positive testimony that
her seat of Government would be in "the isles" it would be an
absurdity to suppose that she did not also occupy the first position
in Naval affairs. Wherever Israel is, the tribe of Dan is still with
her to supply her mariners, and also the tribe of Asher to super-
intend her marine artillery, these were specially trained in mari-
time operations when Israel was in land, and would more fully
develope their training in after years, for be it observed that
nearly the whole of the sea coasts were allotted to the tribeships
of Israel, Judah having no portion of the Mediterranean, but only
a small slip of the Dead Sea Coast, comparatively worthless
for acquiring skill in naval art. This training was not required
from Judah therefore the facilities were not given to her, but
we know Israel did acquire this knowledge; for we are told that
"Hiram sent in the navy his servants, shipmen that had
knowledge of the sea, with the servants of Solomon."

1 Kings, ix. 27, and after her captivity this knowledge would become most important, because when they reached "the isles," and formed their Government, as their people increased, they were to take their surplus population from these islands and make new conquests elsewhere, God promising to "lead them, even by the springs of water shall He guide them." Is. xlix. 10. It is said of Israel, "that his seed shall be in many waters, and his kingdom shall be exalted." Num. xxiv. 7. The Psalmist speaks of God making His way in the sea, and His path in great waters. Ps. lxxvii. 19. Israel is of those who "go down to the sea in ships, and do business in great waters." Ps. cvii. 23. It is Israel that is thus specially commanded, "Sing unto the Lord a new song, and His praise from the end of the earth." And then his Naval power is recognized, for it is said, "Ye that go down to the sea, and all that is therein, the isles, and the inhabitants thereof." Is. xlii. 10. "The enemy shall not exact upon him. * * * "I will beat down his foes before his face." * * * My mercy shall be with him * * * I will set his hand also in the sea, and his right hand in the rivers." Ps. lxxxix. 22-25. THE IDENTITY here is so plain that it is needless to enlarge; all our school children have for ages been taught to laud the supremacy of our Nation in matters of the Navy, and to assign to Britian the favourable position of being Mistress of the Seas, a position that was only to be occupied by Israel, and that is alone occupied by us.

IDENTIFICATION THE EIGHTEENTH.— STOCK BROKING.

I am so anxious to annihilate the very prevalent notion, that Israel in these days refers exclusively to the Church, or professed believers in Christ, that in the present edition of this work I have introduced Stock Broking as an Identity, a function clearly belonging to Israel, but certainly having nothing to do with the rites of a religious service. It is distinctly assigned unto Israel to be the most wealthy Nation upon the face of the earth, and she must be so found. This was a distinguishing privilege from her beginning, and not a single iota of her privileges have been taken from her, but rather added unto. Israel was to acquire such wealth as to be in a position to lend money to every Nation requiring Cash, and who could offer reasonable security for the Loan, no other Nation but Israel was to do this; not only was she to be able to lend to such Nations large sums, but she would be so wealthy as never to require to bor-

row from them, thus we shall find Israel holding a long string
of securities from other Nations, with a long list of loans, bear
ing interest, which in itself would entail almost endless nego-
tiations, ramification of accounts, transfers of stock, settlement
of dividends, and cashing of coupons, for thus is this distinct
promise given to Israel. "For the Lord thy God blesseth
thee, as He promised thee ; and thou shalt lend unto many
Nations, but thou shalt not borrow." Deut. xv. 6. The same
promise is repeated word for word xxviii. 12, and as each separate promise would imply the creation of the needful appara-
tus to give it force, so this promise undoubtedly would call
into being a Stock Exchange, a choice of Investments, a staff
of Stock-brokers, professional Accountants, and Banking operations, settling days and commission agencies, and as nothing
as yet is perfect in the world; from these things would spring
abuses, as well as legitimate uses, that it by no means would
become unreasonable to suppose that we should hear of
" Bulls" and " Bears," " puts" and " calls," and gambling
speculations.

THE IDENTITY simply has to declare that the English
Nation is the only Nation on earth lending to many Nations,
and not requiring to borrow from them. This was only to be
done by Israel, but is alone done by us, and should be sufficient
in itself to establish the Identity. Any Stock-broker would
testify that we lend to all the more powerful Nations, to Russia,
to France, to Austria; and Italy, and some capitalists may remember something about Spanish and Mexican stocks ; reference to any current Stock List, would shew our position. Such
is our wealth, that while the Argentine and Honduras States,
might think they were doing a great thing in borrowing from
us a million, we would think it a very little and immaterial
thing, to make the very trifling mistake of two or three millions
in our Abyssinian accounts. This would be too Lowe an affair
to call forth much comment.

IDENTIFICATION THE NINETEENTH.—
COMPANY OF NATIONS.

Another characteristic under which Israel must be found, is
that of not only having become a Nation, but afterwards having
grown into a Company of Nations; as sure as God's word is
true, so surely must she be found in this position. One of
God's first promises to Abraham was "I will make of thee a
great Nation." Gen. xii. 2. This promise was afterwards
enlarged, thus. "Thou shalt be a father of many Nations."

Gen. xvii. 4. "I will make Nations of thee," Gen. xvii. 6, and it was said unto his wife Sarah "She shall be a mother of Nations." Gen. xvii. 16. This promise was ratified to Jacob, "A Nation and a Company of Nations shall be of thee," Gen. xxxv. 11, and was again passed unto Ephraim, "his seed shall become a multitude of Nations." Gen. xlviii. 19. Again, I protest against the injustice that certain men do to the Bible, when they spiritualize away the literal meaning of these passages. It is not meant that Nations who receive Christ should form a Company of Christian Nations, Abraham would be indignant at this idea; he sent to his own country, and to his own kindred for a wife for his son, that the legitimate seed might be preserved; Sarah said "the son of this bondwomen shall not be heir with my son, with Isaac," and God Himself, to shew that He did not include the Gentile race in these promises, said "in Isaac shall thy seed be called." Gen. xxi. 12. Give but the Bible its true and natural rendering to our people, and it will become as a new book in their hands, full of historic and sacred interest, a book which the masses will delight to study; whereas with the many nonsensical interpretations, rendered by our ministers, it has been divested of interest and put aside. In such a matter as this, let them but see that after Israel was lost, God decreed that they should become a Nation, and a Company of Nations, and their interest would be excited to look for a people upon the face of the earth answering to this description, and would be led to agree with **THE IDENTITY** that our own people was the only people on the Globe that had so become, having formed a "Strong Nation" in Britian, we went forth and formed another in America, another has been formed in Canada, who has her separate Parliament, under her own Prime Minister, for enacting her own Laws, and with the same privileges we find another in Australia, and another in New Zealand, and another in South Africa; these have sprung forth from our own race, without taking into account our Indian possessions, governed by a separate Parliament, and other dependencies, so that we have positively become a Nation, and a Company of Nations. Israel only was to become this; and we are the only Nation on earth that have so become.

IDENTIFICATION THE TWENTIETH.—
THE MEASURING LINE.

Under this heading we present one of the most sublime and powerful proofs of the Majesty and truthfulness of God's sure word, that can be found throughout the entire volume. This alone when it is seen, which it eventually will be, and that shortly, will win the admiration of the entire world. Perhaps more than any other point, it shews that the whole creation, from the very beginning, has been a splendid design, that could only originate in the mind of the Omnipotent, Omnipresent and Omniscient GOD. The Almighty from the very first, foresees from the time that He places our first parents in the Garden, all the Nations and kindreds, that should come forth from them in after ages, He sees the creation of different families, He sees how some would grow into vast multitudes, He decrees how some Nations should rise to great power, and then become extinct, He sees the different locations of separate people on the face of the earth, how single Nations would grow into such multitudes as to defy the power of man to grasp with his intellect any adequate conception of the magnitude. Yet God arranges for the whole, provides their plans, and settled, nearly 6,000 years ago, that for the 800,000,000 of souls or thereabouts, that are now upon the earth, there should be one selected Nation from this mass that should be more highly favored than the rest, and that this one Nation should have such a host of possessions in all parts of the world, not so much situated in the interior of Continents, but along the sea coasts, by the "sides of the earth," so as to form a cord or measuring line, to go right round the globe and enclose or encircle all the other Nations of the world, and for this arduous, superhuman, gigantic undertaking, Israel was selected; it is alone her work, and it is utterly impossible that any other Nation should be found accomplishing it. The character of the work is distinctly told us by Moses, who says "When the Most High divided to the Nations their inheritance. When He separated the sons of Adam, He set the bounds of the people according to the number of the children of Israel. For the Lord's portion is His people, Jacob is the lot (measuring line) of His inheritance." Deut. xxxii. 7-9. This truth is recognized by Jeremiah who in talking about the Gentiles, says "The portion of Jacob is not like them; for he is the former of all things, and Israel is the rod of his inheritance." Jer. x. 16, this is also repeated, Jer. li. 19. "Remember thy congregation which thou hast purchased of old, the rod of thine inheritance which thou hast redeemed." Ps. lxxiv. 2. "I will cause thee to ride upon the high places of the earth, and feed thee with the heritage of Jacob thy father, for the mouth of the Lord hath spoken it." Is. lviii. 14. Thus, this mission given to Israel is a masterpiece of Divine arrangement, an appointment that only could be executed by the Almighty. A matter in which the power, or the will of man is left entirely out of the question, he could not conceive the plan, far more carry it out, so much so, that though plainly told us from the beginning, even Christians among our own people who have made the Bible a life study, have not themselves understood this point; have passed it over with some vague notion, and it is only as the thing is effected, completed, positively accomplished, and seen by us as done, that we are called to come and look, and lost in wonderment and admiration, we cannot but be amazed and convinced of the Supreme Power and Wisdom shewn forth by God. Surely in searching for evidences to the truth of God's word, we want no dead stones dug up from the depth of the earth, for we have but to call forth **THE IDENTITY** and we have living witnesses, speaking masses to testify that His word is true. We are the people that have done this thing. Our Nation have possessions that literally dot round the coasts of the entire world, we only, by our possessions, have become a people that form a boundary line, a cord, or Measuring Line that encircles all the other Nations of the earth; Israel only was to do this, we alone have done it. "On the sceptre of Queen Victoria the sun never sets." "The Queen's morning drum beats all round the world." We not only encompass the earth, but form a complete circle round each Hemisphere. It is a grand fulfillment of prophecy by us, a perfect marvel in itself. We become a living power to prove God's word inspired. Let but the masses be brought to see the speaking splendour of this accomplishment, in its pure and natural signification, apart from the puny interpretation of man, and they could not fail to recognise the Power and the Wisdom of the Creator, and to give their verdict that their entire submission to Him is due. Get a map and trace how literally we have done this thing; take the Eastern Hemisphere, and begin with British Islands, Heligoland, Gibraltar, Malta, Gambia, Sierra Leone, Gold Coast, Lagos, Saint Helena, Cape of Good Hope, Natal, Mauritius, Straits' Settlements, India, Ceylon, Labuan, Western Australia, South Australia, Victoria, Queensland, Tasmania, Hong Kong, and then West Canada, thus completing the circle. The same thing is done round the Western Hemisphere, by our Hudson's Bay territory, Canada, British Columbia, United States (our own race), Islands in the Pacific, New Zealand, Falkland Islands, British Guiana, Trinidad.—Windward Islands.—Grenada, Barbadoes, Saint Lucia, Saint Vincent, Tobago.—Leeward Islands.—Antigua, Montserrat, Saint Christopher, Nevis, Virgin Islands, Dominica, Jamaica, British Honduras, Turks' Islands, Bahamas, Bermuda, United States (east coast), Nova Scotia, Prince Edward Island, New Brunswick, Newfoundland, when we again complete a second circle, which establishes our Identity as indisputable. And writing in the midst of the "rumours of wars," should the great power of the South make conquests rapidly, and should these conquests, instead of being ᵗength become the source of weakness, that in the mighty efforts made, it becomes exhausted in the very climax of success, and thus falls an easy victim into the hands of the King of the North, who in this way would become possessed of the entire Continent of Europe and much of Asia (Palestine excepted). Why! should these arrangements be shortly accomplished, and the life of our Queen be spared, then we should have the literal fulfillment of that remarkable prophecy, "The Lord hath created a new thing in the earth; a woman shall compass a man." Jer. xxxi. 22. But this is merely given as a thought, and is apart from the mission of my work; nevertheless, our Identity, and the "rumours of wars" are cotemporary events.

IDENTIFICATION THE TWENTY FIRST.— THE SPOILER SPOILT.

Another most interesting test in the Identification of Lost Israel, is the fact that there could not now be in existence any Nation who had made war upon her. Israel, in the exercise of her mission, to have lordship over the Gentiles, might be the first to declare war with others, and after having put forth her authority, such Nations might continue in being, but whatever Nation should take upon herself to declare war with Israel, by the sureness of God's word, that Nation should cease to be. This we know to be a fact with those Nations that warred against Israel when she had a political existence, such as the Midianites, Philistines, and others, or the more powerful Nations, such as the Babylonians, and the Assyrians. But God's word is still in force, for the promise was again and again re-delivered to them, after their captivity, for even when she was Lost, Nations would gather against them,"Behold they shall surely gather together, but not by me; whosoever shall gather together against thee shall fall for thy sake; no weapon that is formed against thee shall prosper. This is the heritage of the servants of the Lord." Is. liv. 15 17. "For the Nation and Kingdom that will not serve thee shall perish." Is. lx. 12. "Behold at evening-tide trouble; before the morning he is not. This is the portion of them that spoil us, and the lot of them that rob us." Is. xvii. 14. "Though I make a full end of all Nations whither I have scattered thee, yet will I not make a full end of thee." Jer. xxx. 11. "All they that devour thee shall be devoured; and all thine adversaries, every one of them, shall go into captivity; and they that spoil thee shall be a spoil, and all that prey upon thee, will I give for a prey." Jer. xxx. 16. These are not promises given to Judah, but only to Israel, they become utterly nonsensical when spiritualized; and applied to Churches, after the manner of some of our learned Divines, because cruel infidelity has long made aggressive war upon spiritual truth, and yet is rampant, and if in ignorance we should apply them, to the Jews, we then make them to speak what is untrue, because every Nation now on the earth have fulfilled God's word by oppressing the Jew, and have grown in strength; and it was decreed that Israel herself should war against Judah, for "Manasseh, Ephraim; and Ephraim, Manasseh; they together shall be against Judah." Is. ix. 21. And the time is not now, but is yet to come, when these Two Houses shall cease to vex each other.

THE IDENTITY is most clear upon this point, for our Ancestry, traced to the very spot where Israel was lost, finds our early forefathers under the Assyrian yoke, at the time when that Nation was the most powerful on earth, and from that point to these isles, all the tribeships that History affirms made war with our race, have ceased to be; and when we arrived here the Roman Empire who opposed us, the mightiest Nation the world had then seen, after a lapse of years politically expired; so that now, there does not exist a single Nation who had been the first to spoil us. This cannot be said of any other Nation upon earth, as a reference to the strongest powers will prove; for we ourselves have warred against Russia, and forbad her to take Turkey, and are yet in being. When France was in her prime, we buried her first Emperor in our own ground. Through our troops, we made China open her ports to our trade. This very day we possess Gibraltar, which is a part of Spain. Shewing that we not only exist after having made war with the strongest powers, but have also used the perogative given to Israel, that of having lordship over the Gentiles, and exercising authority upon them, and are the only Nation that have so done.

IDENTIFICATION THE TWENTY-SECOND.— "THE CHURCH OF ENGLAND."

Solomon, who was given to forsee the captivity of Israel, made special entreaties with God concerning this people when Captive, and it is worthy of remark he connects the two great events, the withdrawal of the Latter Rain from the Land, and the Captivity, together; and it is interesting to see that as they went together, so they have returned together, after this

rain has been with-held for hundreds of years, it has only recently been restored, according to promise, and with it the
Identity of Israel, which is surely a certain testimony that it
is God's set time for her discovery. Solomon's petition, accepted
by God, was, that Israel when Captive and given to national
prayer, should in prayer have their faces toward the East.
He says, " When the heaven is shut up, and there is no rain,
because they have sinned against thee; yet if they pray
TOWARD this place, and confess thy name, and turn from
their sin,—then hear thou them from heaven, and forgive the
sin of thy servants, and of thy people Israel, and send rain upon
thy land ; " and further on he says, " If they carry them away
captives unto a land far off, or near, If they return to thee with
all their heart and with all their soul in the land of their captivity, whither they have carried them captives, and PRAY
TOWARD THEIR LAND," &c. 2. Chron. vi. 26 - 38. The
whole chapter is most beautiful and worthy of being read, as it
proves that Israel is a nationality, and in a national capacity,
would be found in prayer with their faces turned toward the
East, which gives us a clear IDENTITY in our own National
Establishment, the Church of England, whose practice has ever
been (though in entire ignorance of our subject) to confess their
sins with their faces turned toward the East, and even in the
burial of the dead the idea is recognized, by the body being en-
tombed with the face turned Eastward, and though this has
been regarded by some sections of the Dissenting Church as
verging upon Superstition, yet it is not; it is a most literal
carrying out of the plan recorded 1. Kings viii, 44, and accepted
by God on our behalf, and should be a standing obligation until
our Captivity is turned, and the Land is restored to us, for this
is the consummation of the arrangement.

Also as to the Architecture of our Churches in the days of
our forefathers ; Mr. Wilson makes the following interesting
remarks " The English Cathedrals appear to have been built
after the fashion of the temples they frequented previous to their
conversion to Christianity. And these Cathedrals, it has been
observed, seem evidently to be built after the design of the
temple at Jerusalem. Like this, they have their most holy
place, the altar; and the holy place, the choir; and the court
outward from thence, for the body of the people ; the more
minute parts and ornaments will, in general, be found to be
exceedingly correspondent."

Do not let me be understood as saying that the Church of
England therefore is the one perfect Church, for she is not.
No Church can be perfect until after our Identity has been
nationally recognized, when God faithfully promises to pour
out His spirit on our seed, and to give us a oneness of heart,

when even our Ritualists will forsake their idols; this is promised, until then, we can "let them alone," for they are childishly powerless. But the Church of England is distinctly recognized in Scripture as a National Establishment, and has only by and bye to make a few alterations, when she will become the most glorious Church ever founded on the earth. Her present description will be found in Ezek. xliii, 7—9. Nearly all the rest, from the 40th chapter to the 12th verse of the 47th, refers to the re-establishment of the Temple service for Judah, but not for Israel, for the Law (Mosaic) is yet to go forth from Zion, and the word of the Lord (the Gospel through Israel) from Jerusalem.

IDENTIFICATION THE TWENTY-THIRD.— FREEMASONRY.

It is not my intention to enlarge upon this heading further than to remark, that Freemasonry has a direct Israelitish origin, and one of the main reasons why the North American Indians and the Nestorians have been reputed to be the descendents of the lost ten tribes, was because a species of Freemasonry was found in their midst. But surely if Freemasonry in the nineteenth century has any head quarters, it is to be found in Britain, and our subject might give to the craft new life and impetus in extending their operations: information on this subject had better be obtained from the Lodges, or from Bro. Geo. S. Kenning, Little Britain.

IDENTIFICATION THE TWENTY-FOURTH.— DRUNKENNESS.

This is a painful Identity, but to bring forth our subject impartially, we must be true, and shew forth the dark side, as well as the bright. Israel must be found with the shame of drunkenness active in her midst: It must be one of her prominent vices, or, if the private interpretation rendered by a large class of the ministry be correct, to wit, that Israel in these days is exclusively the Church, then most surely the Black Cloth must carry the sad signs of debauchery and revelry about with them to a fearful extent, surely it would be a folly with them that Church discipline would not touch, for the Bible infers that this sin in Israel would so largely prevail. But I call upon my readers not to credit the Ministry when they say that Israel is the Church, for she is not, Israel is a nation, distinct from other nations, more highly favoured than France, Russia, Prussia, or any other power, this the Bible declares, which is the safe guide, better than the dictum of any man, whatever reputation for learning he may have. "The Lord hath chosen thee to be a peculiar people unto himself, ABOVE ALL THE NATIONS that are upon the earth" Deut. xiv. 2. "What ONE NATION in the earth is like thy people, even like Israel" 2 Sam. vii. 23. "AN HOLY NATION," 1 Peter ii. 9. and until the promised Spirit be poured upon her after her Identity, Israel, as a distinct nation, would include the good and bad of that nation, and this in a fair and natural way accounts for the drunkenness that prophecy declares would be found in Israel. "Woe to the crown of pride, to the drunkards of Ephraim whose glorious beauty is a fading flower which are on the head of the fat valleys of them that are overcome with wine ! * * *. But they also have erred through wine, and through strong drink are out of the way; the priest and the prophet have erred through strong drink, they are swallowed up of wine, they are out of the way through strong drink, they err in vision, they stumble in judgment." Is. xxviii. 1 - 7. From this we gather that Ephraim is not only given to Ritualism but also to drink, but the "they also" includes Zebulon and Naphtali, Dan and Asher, for these are they "that turn the battle to the gate," and they, like Ephraim, together with Issachar and Reuben of the valleys, would be at times "overcome with wine."

  THE IDENTITY of our nation here surely speaks for itself, drunkenness is a dark page of our national history, it has a world-wide notoriety, it infests all our institutions at home, and perhaps the greatest difficulty that our Missionaries abroad have had to contend against, has been the example set forth to the Gentiles by the drunkards of our own nation, and has severely counter-balanced the good they have sought to effect. And here let me say to our Temperance friends throughout the country, that their organizations, however well arranged, will never eradicate this evil, it will only be overcome by God's own plan, and can alone be effected through the medium of Our Identity, nothing else can remove drunkenness. God himself says so in this very chapter, "IN THAT DAY shall the Lord of hosts be for a crown of glory" instead of "the crown of pride to the drunkards" "By this, therefore, shall the iniquity of Jacob be purged; and this is all the fruit to take away his sin." Is. xxvii. 9. Nothing can be plainer; after our Identity drunkenness will be removed, and we shall be able to use the good gifts from God, instead of abusing them. David, the prophet, more than once says, "WHEN God bringeth back the Captivity of his people, Jacob shall rejoice, Israel shall be glad." Ps. liii. 6. This is AFTER THE IDENTITY, not BEFORE.

IDENTIFICATION THE TWENTY FIFTH.—
FALSE WEIGHTS.

Israel must be found with a section of her people inclined to fraudulent trading, lending themselves to the abominations of false measures, deceitful balances and unjust scales. These are Identities of Israel, and we introduce them that we may make one more effort to destroy the injurious impression that Israel signifies the spiritual Church, for it is manifest that the Church of Christ could have nothing to do with such sins. It is said of Israel "He is a merchant, the balances of deceit are in his hand." Hos. xii, 7. The next verse acknowledges that he had "become rich" by such means. " I have found me out sub-stance," and implying that it was done without offending the legal law: "they shall find none iniquity in me that were sin." "Saying, When will the new moon be gone, that we may sell corn? and the sabbath, that we may set forth wheat, making the ephah small, and the shekel great, and falsifying the balances by deceit?" Amos viii, 5. These are the characteristics of a portion of the trading community in Israel. "Tricks in trade," "clever strokes of business," merchants with "eyes standing out in fatness," given to the "winking of the eye," "speaking with the feet," "teaching with the fingers." God saw all this in Israel after her captivity, and says, "Are there yet the treasures of wickedness in the house of the wicked, and the scant measure that is abominable? Shall I count them pure with the wicked balances, and with the bag of deceitful weights? for the rich men thereof are full of violence." Micah vi, 10. Thus it is evident that the Judgment will record the history of many men in Israel who increased their substance by unrighteousness, Bankers Merchants and Tradesmen who in their day passed as respect-able men, but who at last will testify to the truth of the Scripture that says "The bread of deceit is sweet to a man, but afterwards his mouth shall be filled with gravel," and it is interesting to ob-serve that in the same category are placed the fraudulent merchant and the Ritualistic priest. Israel was punished " be-cause they sold the righteous for silver, and the poor for a pair of shoes." Amos, ii. 6; and after their captivity Isaiah distinctly recognizes the dealer in Ritualism, saying, "The vile person will speak villany, and his heart will work iniquity, to practise hypocrisy, and to utter error against the Lord, and to make empty the SOUL of the hungry." Is. xxxii, 6. Jeremiah was commissioned to say to them, "Woe be unto the pastors that destroy and scatter the sheep of my pasture." xxiii, 1. Ezekiel gives a third testimony against them, "Son of man, prophesy against the shepherds of Israel, prophesy, and say unto them, Thus saith the Lord God unto the shepherds : Woe be to the shepherds of Israel that do feed themselves : should not the shepherds feed the flocks? Ye eat the fat, and ye clothe you with the wool, ye kill them that are fed : but ye feed not the flock." xxxiv, 2, 3.

THE IDENTITY has no obscure corner here, need not speak with an uncertain voice. Surveyors of weights and measures have long been a necessity with us, many tradesmen have reason to hang down their heads with shame as they call to mind their official visits. The very mention of Adulteration would create a world of suggestion. What chapters the Counter might dictate of 11 yards sold for 12, old patterns for new. What tales our County Courts tell of good fish and fruit packed at the top, the rest running down inferior. What a long list many of us could write, of large city Warehousemen, Merchants, Bankers, and Stock Exchange Firms known in our youth, who have succumbed to the principle of the passage which says, "As the partridge sitteth on eggs, and hatcheth them not ; so he that getteth riches, and not by right, shall be a fool." Jer. xvii, 11. Here we have our Railway Directors, curses, instead of blessings, who rob the land of the Sabbath, and pay away their profits in accident compensations. Then as to the passages bearing on the priesthood, they were given to Israel, they must apply to some Class in our midst, they cannot apply to the standard Clergy of the Church of England, they have ever been the salt of our country, rich blessings in our land ; we all have need to thank God for their Evangelical teachings, they have fed the soul, and have not caused "The drink of the thirsty to fail." The standard Clergy of the Church of England have been far better taught than "to utter error against the Lord," nay, those who do thus are our hireling priests, wedded to idols, who impiously accept sacred payment, while they do their utmost to destroy the rich power of a holy, devotional service, by intonation, uncertain nasal sounds, childish, petty, and absurd ceremonials, perverting solemn praise to a brilliant Oratorio, in which the flock can take no part, or reading the Scriptures in an unknown tongue, that they should not be understood. These are our Ritualists : "Ephraim is joined to his idols, let him alone." They might have furnished a separate Identification, but for the fact that God Himself classes them with the swindling tradespeople, "As for them," &c. Ezek. xi, 21. Their power to do harm is "limited," like other Joint Stock frauds : they cannot take us to Rome, simply be-

cause there is no Church of Rome. It had only power to continue forty and two months, or 1260 years, when it was to cease.
God's word is sure, and cannot err. Its power commenced
with the crowning of the first Pope, 606. Add to this the limit
of its time, 1260 years, and we arrive at A.D. 1866. This was
the year of the Infallible man's difficulty, when he ceased to
trust in God, and placed his faith in Napoleon, the year that his
temporal power was wrenched from him, and became embodied
in the might of the French army. From that moment the
Church of Rome ceased to exist, and supplies us with another
proof of God's sure word of prophecy, therefore let not our
nation talk more about Rome, or be anxious about the follies
of those whom God bids us leave alone. They are the " silly
doves of Ephraim," Hos. vii. 11. and will yet return. Hos.
xiv. 8.

IDENTIFICATION THE TWENTY SIXTH.—
OPPRESSION.

I prefer bringing forth this Identity next, though a host of
others crowd upon the mind. I do not find from the prophecies
that any of the national propensities to which Israel were
addicted when in the Land, would depart from her during the
time of her Captivity; on the contrary, Scripture clearly recognises that the same sins would cleave to her in captivity, and
nationally she would not be found willing to forsake them until
the time that her Identity was established; so that the very
Identity of Israel is the instrument that God will use to give
the death blow to many abuses that now afflict His ELECT.
Thus Ritualism, which was with them in the land, and is with
them still, can only be swept from the earth, by the power of
the Identity. But the cruelty of Oppression has far more bane-
ful results upon the masses, it has been to Israel the one great
curse that has checked the full flow of her national prosperity,
and her people's happiness. Her love for using the power of
Oppression was one main reason why she was expelled from the
land, why she forfeited her high estate, and has cost her generations of reproach, toil and misery. " Thus saith the Lord,
for three transgressions of Israel, and for four, I will not turn
away the punishment thereof; because they have sold the righteous for silver, (Ritualism) and the poor for a pair of shoes,
that pant after the dust of the earth on the head of the poor,
and turn aside the way of the meek." Amos. ii. 6. These
sins were not charged against Judah, she had been separately
addressed in previous verses. God not laying the crime of
Ritualism against her, and reference to the Book of Kings will

shew that with but few exceptions, the Kings of Israel "departed not from the sins of Jeroboam, the son of Nebat, who made Israel to sin," (in the ritual service of Baal), whereas on the contrary, the Kings of Judah generally "did that which was right in the sight of the Lord," and Judah to this day cannot be said to oppress her poor, nor does she suffer our poor rates, to be burthened by their keep. Oppression was with Israel, and is so still; it is written against Israel during captivity, "He loveth to oppress." Hos. xii. 7. Of course this is the national and commercial aspect, apart from the religious life, and furnishes another proof that Israel could not be the Church, for it is an impossibility for a Christian to love oppression, those in Israel who are really Christians, are the light of the world, but those who are not in Christ, are still the curse of their brethren: of these God asks "what mean ye that ye beat my people to pieces, and grind the faces of the poor?" Is. iii. 15. "Woe unto them that decree unrighteous decrees, that turn aside the needy from judgment, and take away the right from the poor of my people." Is. x. 2.

THE ENTITY is too apparent; few things have tended so gre   retard our national prosperity, and marred the real happi.... of our people, so much as this love of oppressing others. Exorbitant hours of toil exacted for minimum of pay, testify of it—wealthy City Warehousemen who have more than the heart should desire, pay wicked and starvation prices to their sempstresses, calling forth Tom Hood's sublime protest in his noble and matchless "Song of the Shirt." We have a little nation of ill paid Curates, Clerks, and Workmen, whose principals enjoy princely revenues, and the very luxuries of earth, while their dependents are oppressively struggling in the meshes of poverty, dictating the text "Woe unto him that buildeth his house by unrighteousness, and his chambers by wrong; that useth his neighbour's service without wages, and giveth him not for his work." Jer. xxii. 13. Our Farmers and Agricultural Squires are not exempted from the sin of oppression, as the few shillings doled out to their labourers, and the wretched hovels so many are suffered to live in, testify. God specially addresses the wealthy farmers of Israel, saying, "Behold, the hire of the labourers who have reaped down your fields, which is of you kept back by fraud, crieth." James v. 4. Oppression is in us and permeates through all society, our very governments have been oppressed by the people, the people by the governments, and so forth. How shamefully is this exemplified by our treatment of paupers—homeless poor, like felons, are handed over to the supervision of the police when they want a night's shelter, and have to file outside the railing of a police station, that passers-by might gaze upon their misery, submit to the rough questions of the Inspector, at times passed long distances to a workhouse, to undergo cross questioning by Officials of another stamp, and then have to pay by labour, seven times the value of the accommodation. All this is a grave mistake, by which the full prosperity of our Nation has been hindered; we have wealth in our Country, and could have multiplied it a hundred fold (but for this dark blot), resulting in almost universal contentment among the masses of the people. It is our own fault that we have pauperism, a consequence of Oppression. God has declared, and His word is sure; that He did not intend much poor to be in our midst, that He wished so to bless our English Nation that there should be times when we should have no poor at all. Deut. xv. 4. He has made special provision for us against poverty, not having done the same to any other nation, and if we had carefully hearkened to his voice, pauperism would have been unknown to us, we suffer from it through our sin; every department of trade is crippled, railway receipts are dwarfed, and poor rates form a millstone about our necks, simply because we have not properly used the provision God has made. God gave to us our Colonies expressly to prevent pauperism, the 49th of Isaiah is nothing more than a chapter of English History, entirely without point or meaning, if applied to any other people. It contains the Charter of our Colonial Office, the history of our Colonies; addresses us in these " Isles," tells us they had become too small for us, " by reason of the inhabitants," because we had the multitudinous seed in us. We ourselves in the 20th verse, cried out for some new country, for more room, saying " the place is too strait for me : give place to me that I may dwell," this was Israel suffering the inconvenience of an overcrowded country, and in the same chapter God tells us He had heard the prayer, that the request was granted, that He had provided for us the " desolate heritages," and we have before seen that all the waste heritages that were then existing, are now in our possession. Had we made use of them in the way God intended we should have done, we should be entirely without workhouses in our land, Philanthropy would amply have provided for all the Charity needed. We should have sent forth our surplus populage to till these waste lands; but Oppression has kept them at home, that the labour market might be overstocked, and labour become cheap, and this is why our wealthy Manufacturers, Farmers, and large employers of labour, are generally found decrying down Emigration, they know that to thin the country, means the raising of wages; would enforce them at last to pay honestly; so they meanly and subtlely pretend to oppose Emigration upon humane grounds. The time has now come to sweep this cant away; grave times are ushered in. These are the latter days; the wars have commenced; the fullness of the Gentiles have set in; the injunction has been obeyed, to preach the gospel as a witness to every nation; the Latter Rain has been restored; knowledge runs swiftly to and fro; and, ISRAEL IS FOUND. These are the great proofs of latter day times. Now, we are about to enjoy a season of refreshing and quiet, a few years of rest, with a thorough immunity from the troubles that will beset the other nations; but still Armageddon is before us; it is coming upon us; we cannot avert it; it may be 100 years before it comes; it may be sooner. It is the time of our trouble; we are the Elect; and for our sakes alone it is promised these days shall be shortened. It is the time that "wheresoever the body is, thither will the eagles be gathered together." The time that God will avenge Israel "His own elect," the time when the entire armies of the Continent shall be gathered against us, suggesting Christ's question, "nevertheless when the son of man cometh, shall he find faith on the earth? This question has no manner of reference to truth. We are positively assured that there will be hundreds of millions of sincere, Christ loving and expecting souls at this time, but it means shall we, the elect nation, the Israel, after all God's marvels done for us, shall we with the earth against us, with all the modern appliances of skilled warfare before us, have faith in the promise that we shall prevail? Victory will be ours, but will be obtained for us, more by our Colonies than by ourselves. It is the young lions that come forward. Ezek. xxxviii. 13. The tidings out of the east and out of the north, shall trouble Gog. Dan. xi. 44. Hence the importance of developing our Colonies. Every workhouse is a reproach to us; each represents a town of wasted strength; an army extracted from us. Instead of herding our poor in physical weakness, in these nests of infamy, had we sent them forth to till the wastes and beautify God's earth, we might have had hundreds of new towns for the commerce of Old England to supply. They would have become a blessing to us, not a curse; a strength, not a weakness; but the advocate of cheap labour, says, "Utopian!" Believe him not; every town formed is the result of first settlers. New York, Quebec, Adelaide, Wellington and Cape Town, with all the others, testify against him. What has been done, can be repeated, and there is yet ample room to duplicate the whole. Keeping up our ratio of population, which we shall; in 100 years hence our race will have increased to 300,000,000, what will become of England unless we make the proper use of our blessings, let hateful Oppression no longer stand in the way; let the Nation insist that Government take Emigration in hand; let our workhouses be emptied, and free passages with grants be made; then shall we have a Government attending to the real well being of the people, and not until then. God never enjoined upon us the duty of supporting the able bodied man; He only commissions us to take care of the stranger, the widow and the fatherless; for the widower, and the motherless, provision is made, if not in England, in our immense possessions; but having made the mistake by discouraging emigration, and wasting national strength, through the horrors and immorality always resulting from overcrowding. It becomes our duty to rectify this mistake, by providing from the national purse, sufficient to enable these impoverished ones, comfortably to settle in the countries God Himself has given them. The same amount of money we threw away, over ten of our people in Abyssinia, without any "value received," applied in this direction, would be a stroke of real statesmanship, and directly, and sensibly benefit the whole of the country. If the people willed it, no earthly power could hinder it. Heaven would not oppose, because it grieves that it has not been done before.

IDENTIFICATION THE TWENTY SEVENTH.— "BLINDNESS IN PART."

Perhaps one of the most marvellous incidents connected with the history of Israel since they were lost, is that of their "Blindness," their utter ignorance of themselves, it is said of them "His watchmen are blind, they are all ignorant." Is. lvi. 10. They were to accomplish all the wonderful works given to Israel; yet they were not to know themselves, were to be forgetful of the rock that begat them, Paul calls this a mystery and says "I would not, brethren, that ye should be ignorant of this mystery, lest ye should be wise in your own conceits, that blindness in part is happened to Israel, until the fulness of the Gentiles be come in." Rom. xi. 25. In the first verse he glories in being "an Israelite," "of the tribe of Benjamin," and speaks only of Israel, and not of Judah, when he asks "Hath God cast away His people?" And refers to Israel as being the elect Nation, and not a Church, when he says "God hath not cast away His people which He foreknew." He had the authority of Scripture for saying this; for God Himself had said "they shall be as though I had not cast them off." Zech. x. 6. Yes, even in this blind state, they should be the favoured people, not for their own goodness, but that the faithful promises made, should stand; for Paul says "Israel hath not obtained that which he seeketh for; but the ELECTION hath

obtained it, and the rest were blinded." Rom. xi. 7. By "the
rest," he referred to the nine tribes who had been carried into
captivity by Assyria—the bulk of the nation—for in the two
previous verses he spoke only of the remnant that had been
preserved, and who in the time then present—the days of
Paul—were Christians, not having given themselves to the
service of Baal, just as the seven thousand men in the days of
Elijah had been lovers of truth, and proof against the wickedness of ritualism. This remnant did not belong to Judah, but
to Israel; being of Benjamin, that one tribe especially left behind to carry out Christ's work in the days of the Apostles.
1 Kings xi. 13 and 36. "The rest," i.e.—the nation of Israel,
were "blinded," but yet as a Nation they were fore-ordained,
pre-destinated, elected to fulfil all the missions given to them.
Hence the Apostle says, it was not so much they that per-
formed them, for they "were blinded," but "the election."
God speaking of Israel, says "I will bring the blind by a way
they knew not; I will lead them in paths they have not known,
•   •   •   These things will I do unto them, and not forsake
them. •   •   •   Who is blind but My servant? •   •   •
Who is blind as he that is perfect, and blind as the Lord's
servant? Seeing many things, but thou observeth not." Is.
xlii. 16-19. And surely THE IDENTITY can testify to
this fact. We have established by Twenty Seven Identities, the
Indentification of the English with Israel, and could yet bring
forward as many more if needed. We have proved that we
are the only nation that have brought forth their works, that
there is not a single flaw, not a link missing, that we have
without one exception accomplished all, whereas no other
nation has touched them, and now by no possibility whatever
could do so, and yet hitherto we have been blind to this fact,
notwithstanding the remarkable coincident, that we have as a
nation, been confessing for ages, through the Common Prayer
Book of the Church of England, that we were positively, and
literally Israel, as the following quotations prove. "O God,
we have heard with our ears, and our fathers have declared
unto us the noble works thou didst in their days, and in the old
time before them." "He remembering His mercy, hath holpen
His servant Israel, as He promised to our forefathers, Abraham
and his seed for ever." Surely nothing could be plainer than
that "blindness in part" has happened to us, it has been designed by God that it should have been so, but He also designs
that it should be removed, and is now about to make most
valuable use of this blindness. It is now specially to serve
the welfare of the Church, our dear Redeemer's Kingdom, for
while some men in their zeal to confirm the truth of Christianity, have been eager to establish Christian Evidence

Socities, Exploration Funds, and have been digging in the bowels of the earth for inscription stones, collecting anything that could in the slightest degree testify to Bible truth, God himself designs to bring forth living testimony; He intends through the medium of our "blindness" to destroy Infidelity; that while Tom Payne, and his school have been asserting "there is no God," we are to be called forth, and invested with the sublime mission, to testify that there is a God, and that our God is God; a holier, more heaven born mission could not be given to any people, it is alone given to our nation, for God now says to us—to us, the so-called English, but now identified as Israel, "Bring forth the blind people that have eyes, • • • let them bring forth their witnesses that they may be justified. • • • Ye are my witnesses, saith the Lord, and my servant whom I have chosen ; that ye may know, and believe me, and understand that I AM HE; before me there was no God formed, neither shall there be after me; I, even I, am the Lord ; and beside me there is no Saviour. • • • Ye are my witnesses, saith the Lord, THAT I AM GOD." Is. xliii. 10-12. Christians! if no other purposes were served by our Identification, surely this one alone should fire our souls with living zeal to effect its national acknowledgment. Ye that love the Lord, is it nothing to you that God's character should be vindicated? We are this "blind people," that have to be brought forth. It is God's own adopted means of certifying to truth; the only method that can prevail, and effect the purpose; waste not valuable time, and insult not your God, by resorting to your own judgment, and using your own appliances, but obey God, do as He bids you, bring Israel to the front, "bring forth the blind people," establish our Identity, for this is the only power that will be used by God, to bring the Gentile Nations to be willing to be taught of the Lord, and receive salvation through our Lord and Saviour Jesus Christ. The word of the Lord has said this; remember God works by the use of means; we must shew our anxiety for this to be done, before He will do it. "Thus saith the Lord God; I will yet for this, be enquired of by the house of Israel, to do it for them." Ezek. xxxvi. 37. "Ye that make mention of the Lord, keep not silence. And give Him no rest, till He establish, and till He make Jerusalem a praise in the earth." Is. lxii. 7.

Christians, this matter is now fairly in your hands, it is a new power for you to use, for the glory of God, the salvation of souls, and the welfare of our individual Nation. I leave you accountable to God, for the way you make use of this power, and to Him be all the Glory, now, and ever. Amen. (I have said.)

———————

POSTSCRIPT.

Our Divines often tell us how easy it is to build theories upon individual, and isolated passages of Scripture, and are most choice with their advice, that we should be careful to compare Scripture with Scripture. This has been an anxious study—from between two and three hundred texts that have been advanced, not one has been used to bear upon Israel that was not given to her, and her alone, without having any bearing upon Judah ; also, the passages brought forward to distinguish Judah, only refer to her, and not to Israel. For each single text supplied, at least ten others could be brought forward having direct substantiating testimony ; indeed very much of the Bible could be reproduced. So that, if ever a subject has been introduced adhering to the rule of comparing Scripture with Scripture, surely this subject has in the most copious manner.

NOTICE !

Price 6d. ; post-free, 7d. 88 pages.

FLASHES OF LIGHT,
By Edward Hine.
BEING THE SECOND PART
TO THESE
"Twenty-seven Identifications of the English Nation with Lost Israel."

CONTAINING

Three Chapters by the Rev. F. R. A. GLOVER, M.A., upon "Jacob's Stone," now under our Coronation Chair; author of "England, the Remnant of Judah," &c.

Three Chapters by PROFESSOR SMYTH, F.R.S.S., L. and E., the Astronomer Royal for Scotland, of Edinburgh University, &c. Author of "Life and Work at the Great Pyramid," &c.

One Chapter by CAPTAIN CARTER, Professor of Sanskrit, Cheltenham College ; AND SHOWING

THAT ENGLAND—
Is the ONLY Nation preserved by God's Oath.
Can never be Defeated.
Is NOT in need of a large Standing Army.
Can never become a Republic ; because her Monarchy is IRREMOVEABLE.
Has a Queen lineally descended from the Royal House of David.

The Teutonic Difficulty ; "They are not all Israel that are of Israel ; " Seven Eighths of the Bible generally misunderstood; The Case of Judah; Everlasting Punishment; Seventeen New Identities;"Neither Jew nor Greek;" "Spiritual Israel," an unscriptural phrase; The Irish; Weights and Measures; The Battle of Dorking; A Layman's Sermon; The Tribe of Benjamin, &c.

ANNOUNCEMENTS.

This Work has not been advertised, and the author has studiously refrained from soliciting Reviews; notwithstanding within eight months, some 16,000 have been sold, which is a sufficient evidence of the interest it has excited in the public mind; and the very numerous correspondence it has elicited, testifies that the subject is held to be a most important one.

The Author desires to add to this interest by the Delivery of LECTURES in town or country, his services in this way being rendered gratuitously, requiring the payment of expenses only. Independent of the great advantages and additional interest imparted to the subject by an Oral Delivery, a Lecture affords the opportunity for explanations upon points that the Book itself cannot touch, and in many instances this has proved highly satisfactory.

THREE LECTURES are prepared, which could form a course, or be delivered separately, viz :—

The Identity of the English Nation with the Lost House of Israel.

The Importance of Emigration, founded upon the theory that the English are Lost Israel.

The Political, Social, and Religious Uses of the fact that the English People are the Lost Tribes of Israel.

Intimation has been received that this work has been introduced for study amongst Sunday School Teachers, Adult Bible Classes, and Young Mens' Associations. The Author would willingly meet these Students, when objections might be solved, fresh information afforded, and the study of years be found advantageous.

The Author is also willing to answer, to the best of his ability, any questions that may be sent to him; an immense number of letters have been received, which have been answered in rotation.

If friends wishing replies would kindly enclose an addressed *Stamped* Envelope, they would oblige.

All communications to be addressed to MR. EDWARD HINE, 73, Little Britain, London, E.C.

Price will not exceed 4s. **IN THE PRESS.** Ps. 300.

WE SEE NOT OUR SIGNS.—Psalm lxxiv. 9.

ENGLAND

THE REMNANT OF JUDAH, AND THE ISRAEL OF EPHRAIM AND MANASSEH.

Look unto the Rock whence ye are hewn, and to the Hole of the Pit whence ye are digged; look unto Abraham your Father, and unto Sarah that bare you. Isa. li. 1.

And it shall come to pass, that in the place where it was said unto them, Ye are not My People, there shall it be said unto them, Ye are the sons of The Living God. Hos. i. 10.

And they are the Ten Thousands of Ephraim, and they are the Thousands of Manasseh. Gen xlviii. 19; Deut. xxxiii. 17; Gen. xlviii. 20.

NEW EDITION, much added to, long prepared, NOT RE-WRITTEN.

By Rev. F. R. A. GLOVER, M.A.,

LATE CHAPLAIN TO H.M.'S CONSULATE AT COLOGNE.

SOME TIME RECTOR OF CHARLTON-IN-DOVER.

LONDON:

CRUSE & CO.

MDCCCLXXI.

" We cannot venture to give so much as a guess at the extent of change " which this discovery, if verified, must produce in the whole scheme of Scrip-" ture Prophecy hitherto in vogue; or, at the marvellous amount of light, it will " throw over the political aspect of the present times." *The Press*, Nov. 16, 1861.

" *If* verified " " The surest and best characteristics of a well-founded and " extensive induction is, when verifications of it spring up, as it were, spon-" taneously into notice, from quarters where they might be least expected; or, " from among instances of that very kind, which were, at first, considered hos-" tile. Evidence of this kind is irresistible, and compels assent with a weight that " scarcely any other possesses." *Sir J. Herschel, Nat. Phil.* p. 170.

" Isaiah lv. 10. seems to enounce, as a Principle, that the Lord *swears* that " no Prediction, or Oracle of His, shall fail of its Object, or of enlightening *some* " in the very Age, for whose Use it was sent. If so, and no Person noted a " Fulfilment of this in the last past century, we must conclude that it had no " Fulfilment, and was not given for that Age." *Wolff's Researches*, 1835.

Questions* which deeply affect the whole human
Race: particularly the Moslem[1] and the Hindu;[2] but,
primarily, the Hebrew[3] and the British Races.[4]

"The Heart of the Righteous studieth to answer: but the Mouth of the
Wicked poureth out evil things."   Prov. xv, 28.

1. Where is The Perpetual Sceptre of Judah ?[4]   Gen. xlix. 10.
2. Where is The Indestructible Throne of David ?[4]   Jer. xxxiii. 17.
3. Where, SHILOH not having been manifested, floats The Standard
     of the Tribe of Judah ?[4]   Gen. xlix. 10.
4. Where is the Pillar of Witness, Jacob's Pillow ?[4] Ib. xxviii. 22.
5. To what Rejected Stone did David refer in the Hymn as the
     procession wound up the Hill of Jebus, to consecrate the
     Threshing-Floor of Araunah ?[3][5][4]   Ps. cxviii. 22.
6. Where is The Favoured Remnant of Judah ?[4]   Jer. xv. 11.
7. Where is The Daughter of the Dispersed ?[1][2]   Zeph. iii. 10.
8. Where was the Kingdom New-Planted, of Jeremiah ? Jer. i. 10 ?
9. Where is The Offering she is to bring ?[3] Is. xi. 12. Zeph. iii. 10.
10. What is The Reserve which is to be pardoned ?[3]   Jer. l. 20.
11. Where is Ephraim, The Multitude of Nations ?[4]   Gen. xlviii. 19.
12. How can Judah's Pre-eminence and Abiding Sceptre and Jo-
     seph's Universal Dominance co-exist ?
          Gen. xlviii. 8—10 ; xlviii. 24-5-6. Deut. xxxiii. 15-6-7.
13. Where is Ephraim,[4] with which Judah[3] is to choose one Head ?
     Is. xi. 13.   Hos. i. 10.
14. Where the Ephraim and Manasseh, in whom Israel is to pro-
     nounce blessing ?   Gen. xlviii. 20.
15. How are the Two Families to be united ?[3][4]   Jer. xxxiii. 24.
16. What is The Pure Language, in which the Daughter of the
     Dispersed,[4] and, The [Lord's] Offering[3] which she is to bring,
     are to consent, with all the people,[13] to serve the Lord ?
                                                       Zeph. iii. 9, 10.
17. Where are they to choose "One Head ?"[4]   Hos. i. 10.
18. What is, and where the Place of, The Day of Jezreel ?
                                           Hos. i. 10. Jer. xxxi. 27—38.
19. What is The Israel of Blessing,[3][4] which is to be "A Third"
     with Egypt[1] and Assyria ?[1][3]   Is. xix. 24, 25.

"Cast thy bread upon the waters: for thou shalt find it after many days."
Eccl. xi. 1.

"It is a duty never to intermit the assertion of an important truth ;
because, though we may not dare to hope that it will be at once recognized, it may, nevertheless, so prepare the minds of others, as to
produce at some time future, greater impartiality of judgment, and the
consequent triumph of light"—*Silvio Pellico*. *Le mie prigione*,
Cap. xxi. p. 58, *ed.* 1848.

---

* Questions, which find their solution in the Argument of this Book—see p. 3
—an extract from the Introduction of the First Edition, 1861, p. 7. They were
put into circulation, in this form, in various languages, ten years since, 5, 8, 12,
and 14, excepted.

Of these conjectures this is the sum, viz.—

1. That England is the Possessor and *rightful* Owner of the Stone of Jacob,* called Jacob's Pillow; now used as the Coronation Throne:† "a Pillar of Witness," consecrated by the Patriarch some 3600 years since.† Gen. xxviii. 18—22:—

2. That England is, in her Royal Family, of the Stem of Jesse; and, being so, is, as the Hereditary Holder of the Perpetual Sceptre and Inheritor of the Standard of Judah, the fostered Remnant of Judah :[1]—

3. That *Angle*-land, in her origin, and descent of her people, is, in her own position, the reality of Joseph; and, in that of her colonies,[2] the Ephraim of Jacob, *i. e.* the Israel of Ephraim :—

4. That, in this COMBINATION of the TWO FAMILIES,[3] there has been a *commencement* of the fulfilling of the prophecy which foretells the Union of these Two Elements of the World's approaching Future ;[4] —the prediction that Judah shall not vex Ephraim, nor, Ephraim, envy Judah :—by which COMBINATION, also, England is qualified to be, Standard-Bearer of *All*-Israel :—and that

5. Herein, is involved the responsibility of action which is clearly pointed out, as the privilege of the Israel of Blessing, in Isaiah xix.: that pleasant instrument of a happy future to "Egypt, the (Mohammedan), God's people," and "Assyria (the Hindu and Buddhist), the work of God's hands ;" as "THE THIRD "[5] of sanctification to the other TWO-THIRDS ; and the incipient development of the accomplished promises of GOD to "Israel, his Inheritance," viz. England: the now living real descendants and representatives of Abraham, Isaac, and Jacob.

[1] Jer. xv. 11.   [2] Gen. xlviii. 19.   [3] Jer. xxxiii. 24.   [4] Isa. xi. 13.   [5] Isa. xix. 24.

* "It has continued," says Dean Stanley, "probably the chief object of attraction to the innumerable visitors of the Abbey." *Memorials of Westminster Abbey.*

† "To my eye," says Professor Ramsay, who analysed the Stone by desire of the Dean of Westminster, ' it appears as if it had been originally prepared for building purposes, but had never been used." The Very Rev. the Dean later goes on to say:—

‡ "It is the one primeval monument which binds together the whole Empire. The Iron Rings, the battered surface, the crack which has all but rent its solid mass asunder, bear witness to its long migrations. It is, thus, imbedded in the heart of the English monarchy ; an element of poetic, patriarchal, heathen times, which like Araunah's rocky threshing floor in the midst of the Temple of Solomon, carries back our thoughts to races and customs now almost extinct: a Link, which unites the Throne of England with the traditions of Tara and Iona,"—AND, NO LESS, OF JERUSALEM AND BETHEL,—"and connects the charm of our complex civilization with the forces of our Mother Earth, the stocks and stones of savage nature." *Ib.* 67.

From the Preface to the New Edition.

"And, as concerning ' Combinations,' let him who is great in the science of Computation of Chances, declare the arithmetical value of any hypothesis, which shall command in amount, the number to one, which the combinations, here brought into coincidence, create and justify, to favour the presumption of the truth of the hypothesis assumed in this book. Then will its Compiler and the Rabbi of...... also, no doubt, willingly accept his counter-hypothesis when examined and proved. In May, 1861,......"Do any of your people believe in this matter that you have brought to my notice ?" said the Rabbi to me. "No," said I, "not one." "What do they *say* to it ?" "Some

think me mad : others, a fool." "Well," said he, "with respect to
"the Stone, all that I have to say, is, that I have never heard of any-
"thing, concerning it, half so reasonable as that of which you have
"now told me. And, as to the entire hypothesis, when those who
"take upon themselves to oppose what you have to allege, have any
"consistent theory to produce which shall account for the existence
"of all these things in combination, which you have brought to the
"surface, and, so as to agree with History and not to oppose the due
"requirements of Holy Writ, it will be time to take their view of the
"case into consideration." "For my part," he added, "I wholly
accept it." And, he subsequently ejaculated, "Es ist der Eckstein
der Zukünft." And, when I told him that I was glad to hear *him*
say so,—not, said I, that it makes me believe one whit the more that
it is so, because you have said it, but because you *see* it; especially,
because you are a Jew, and still more, because you are a Rabbi,......
he added, emphatically, "Yes, it is! It *is* certainly the Corner-Stone
of the Future!" "Ya, das *ist* es! Es *ist*, gewiss, der Eckstein der
Zukünft !" And when I parted from him later, the result of his six
weeks thought and reflection—the interval between my first and my
last interview with him—was given in his last words to me, in allusion
to the accompanying paper, and in especial to its third question,
"Where, SHILOH not having been manifested, floats the Standard of
the tribe of Judah ?"......" Nehmen Sie acht, Herr Pastor! Nehmen
Sie acht ! *Ich bin bereit das Panier zu tragen*." "Give heed, Rev.
Sir. Mind what I say ! *I* am ready to carry the Standard !" *What
Standard?* Necessarily, "the Standard" in the sense in which I had
used the phrase in the Question, No. 3, above. Date 1801.

Strange that a German Rabbi and an English press-writer should
have so curiously concurred in their practical conclusion on the subject; as from the already given extract from "*The Press*," it is evident
that they do. P. 1.

And as another learned Rabbi said to me, "If your book is true, that
is the book for the Jew ! I am *convinced* that there is *much* in it."

"Of such momentous consequence is the subject," as deems a
valued and deep-thinking friend, that "nothing of such crucible importance has occurred within the Sees of Canterbury and York since
they were founded."

Thanks be to GOD, I have lived to see, that, working, as I did,
against well-founded anticipations of widely-extended ridicule, even
thus, this book has not been put forth in vain. And now again, it
has been brought before a thoughtful public, in a manner altogether
unknown to me ; but such, as to call the attention of thousands of
earnest minds to an intelligent consideration of the promisses. That
their conclusior may be as holy as it shall be true, is the prayer of
the unworthy Servant of the Temple, who has felt it right to set the
case before them ; and, now, in re-iterating it, to make it clearer, by
the light of new evidence flashing out of old things.

If such was my conviction as to the small amount of sympathy that
my utterances were likely to command, should any ask, why I ven-
tured in standing alone, to run counter to the prudent conclusions of
all my fellows, I can only say, that I felt what has been expressed so
much better by another than I can deliver it for myself, that I am
glad to take advantage of his formula to close the Preface to this
Edition. *Silvio Pellico, as in* p. 2.